Famous Men of
Modern Times

Illustrated

By John Henry Haaren
and A. B. Poland

Copyright © 2020 by Cedar Lake Classics

ISBN: 978-1-61104-701-1

Publisher: Cedar Lake Classics

Table of Contents

Preface

IT should be carefully noted that this little volume is the fourth and last in a series written for the express purpose of creating a deeper interest in the study of History.

These four volumes are entitled respectively "Famous Men of Greece;" "Famous Men of Rome;" "Famous Men of the Middle Ages;" and "Famous Men of Modern Times."

The very titles of these books convey at once, both to the teacher and the pupil, that the method of teaching History here pursued is by approaching it through the realm of Biography; and it is not too much to say that, in this respect, the previous volumes have been eminently successful.

There is something in life that makes its own personal appeal to life. The living man—be he soldier, sailor, statesman or hero—forms a fixed and abiding center around which the pupil can gather the prominent events of the country to which the man belongs.

The Conquest of Granada, without the presence and interest of Ferdinand and Isabella; the Discovery of America, without the life story of Christopher Columbus; the splendid achievements of Galileo and Newton, apart from the thrilling incidents in the lives of the men who made them; or the mere record of the winning of Italian Independence or of our own Civil War, without some knowledge of Garibaldi and Lincoln; these will not long endure in the mind of the average pupil. But when coupled with the story of the sufferings and struggles, the sorrows and the joys, of the men who were the living heart and soul of these movements, the narratives become infinitely more fascinating, and take a deeper hold upon the mind, memory and heart of each individual student; and this holds true throughout the entire series.

It has been forcibly pointed out in the preface to the earlier volumes of this series, that "the child almost unconsciously identifies himself with these great heroes of the past, finds himself imagining what he would do if placed in a like position, and living their lives over again in his own."

There can be no quicker method of gaining the pupil's attention, and no surer way of holding it, than that which is here attempted; and this is but another way of saying that there is not, and cannot be, any truer or better method of acquainting young people with the great facts of history than that which gives to them a knowledge of the men by whom the history has been made.

The numerous and beautiful illustrations running through all these books will also be of real help in this respect.

The study of history through biography is as natural as is the attainment of growth and strength through the use of proper and nourishing food. The one is the logical outcome of the other.

To feel the thrill of life in history destroys all the dryness and tedium of the study, and is a valuable help to teacher and pupil alike.

These books, following the recommendations of the foremost educators of our times, have been prepared with this end in view; and it is both hoped and believed that they will serve this useful purpose.

Acknowledgments are due from the authors to the Rev. W. F. Markwick, D. D., for valuable assistance in editing and revising the manuscript and in reading the proofs.

CHAPTER 1

Lorenzo the Magnificent

(1449-1492)

THE thousand years between the downfall of the Roman Empire and the Discovery of America are called the Middle Ages—which means the ages between ancient and modern times.

This was a very stormy period. In the early part, the barbarians overran Europe and destroyed almost every sign of civilization. They were brought under some control through the efforts of the Church, and, as time advanced, there was progress in the arts of civilized life.

Schools were established in monasteries, and here and there in large cities, but there was no general popular education as we consider it now. This is not so strange, for there were no printed books.

The printing press had not been invented; all books at that time were manuscripts, that is they were written by hand, for that is what the word manuscript means. They were written on parchment, which was sheepskin specially prepared so that it would take ink.

Of course books written by hand were expensive, for it took a great deal of time to write them. Most of the people in Europe, therefore, lived and died without ever having a book in their hands. In only a few of the largest cities and monasteries was it possible to find a library containing as many as five hundred volumes.

When at length the printing press was invented, the desire for knowledge became widely spread. People felt that they must have books to read, and to study. They saw the necessity for schools in which their children might be taught.

Of all the countries of Europe none was more thoroughly awakened than Italy; and among the places that were thus aroused to a desire for knowledge of all kinds, one of the first was the city of Florence. Florence early became the home of many learned men, and no city did more for the enlightenment of Europe than she.

Here lived the famous family of the Medici (med' e chee). For several generations the Medici had been engaged in what was then almost the only commerce of the world. This was trade with India. Caravans of camels brought silks and shawls, spices and precious stones from the far East to the shores of the Mediterranean. Ships transported them to Florence. Trains of pack horses and mules carried them from Florence across the passes of the Alps to the cities of northern and western Europe.

This traffic had made the Medici very wealthy; and not only wealthy but powerful. For three hundred years the family ruled the city and people of Florence. But it was not their wealth alone that gave them their power. Their political influence based on industrial conditions was great also.

The city was, like ancient Athens, a state. It made its own laws, and had the right to coin its own money; it made war or peace with foreign countries.

The government of the state was republican. But Florence was one of the strangest little republics that ever existed. It had this peculiar law, that no man should hold the office of chief magistrate, unless he belonged to one of the guilds, or "arts" as they were called.

These were about the same as our modern trades unions. But the Florentines had even more such unions than we have. Not only were there unions of carpenters and masons and others who worked with their hands, the people who worked with their heads were also united. There were "arts" or unions of the bankers, the merchants, the doctors, and the lawyers.

From the members of the "arts" the Florentines chose their officers. The government of the city was vested in the "Great Council of Nine." These Nine consisted of seven who were head workers, and two who were hand workers. This arrangement brought those who worked with their heads and those who worked with their hands very close together. It caused the lawyers and merchants and bankers to have a friendly feeling for the carpenters and masons and others who made their living by "the sweat of their brows;" and no man could long be ruler in Florence who did not love the working people.

The Medici family were famed for doing good with their money among the people of Florence. And therefore one after another of them found it easy either to be made the "standard-bearer" as the president of the republic was called; or to have men put into office who would carry out his wishes. In 1449, just about the time when Europe was preparing to enter upon a period of renewed activity, one of the Medici line was born who was named Lorenzo. He died in 1492, the very year in which Columbus discovered America.

His grandfather, Cosimo de Medici had given many fine buildings to Florence, among which was its famous cathedral.

Lorenzo's father had also spent immense sums of money for the benefit of Florence. He had been really the ruler of the city for many years, although he very seldom held the office of standard-bearer, or had any official title.

When he died the people of Florence desired that another Medici should manage the republic, and therefore they invited Lorenzo to do for them as his father had done. He accepted their invitation, and became their ruler.

He proved to be much like the famous Athenian, Pisistratus—a tyrant who was not tyrannical. He ruled for the welfare of the people. He did not think that the first duty of a good ruler was to make his people soldiers.

He saw that the best thing to be done for the Florentines was to enlighten them—to furnish them with books and schools.

But where were books to be procured? There were monasteries in various parts of Europe in which were large numbers of books; and among these were manuscripts of many works of the old Greeks and Romans. But the principal hiding-place of manuscripts, especially those of Greek writers, was Constantinople. And it happened in a very strange way that the books of Constantinople were at that very time being brought to Western Europe.

The inhabitants of Constantinople were Greeks. They read the writings of Homer and Plato, and the Gospels and Epistles of the New Testament, in the original Greek.

The Turks who had long been menacing the city cared nothing for Homer and Plato; and they hated the books of the New Testament. They thought that men needed no book but the Koran of Mohammed. Many of them believed that no one ought to read any other book.

Lorenzo the Magnificent

At length, in 1453, Constantinople was actually taken by the Turks, and a great number of its people escaped and went forth to seek new and peaceful homes in Western Europe. Many went to Italy; and of these, several found their way to Florence.

Some of these men brought manuscripts with them; and they told their new Italian friends that others might be obtained in Constantinople.

After this the Medici, and men like them, carried on for years a diligent search for books. They sent men to the monasteries of Italy, Germany, and England, and to Constantinople to purchase whatever ancient manuscripts they could find. One of those who went to the old Eastern capital brought back two hundred and thirty-eight, among which were the writings of Plato and Xenophon, who lived in Athens four hundred years before Christ.

Lorenzo caused many of the old manuscripts to be copied; and, what was better, he had them printed. For just before Lorenzo's birth, Gutenberg had perfected his printing press; and, three years after Lorenzo was born, the first book printed in Florence had made its appearance. It was an edition of Vergil, the great Latin poet; and very likely Lorenzo used a copy of it when he studied Latin.

He lived to see books wonderfully multiplied. By the time he was thirty years old, Vergil and Horace, Homer and Xenophon could be printed so cheaply that they were bought for school boys.

Like other merchant princes of the time, Lorenzo established a famous school in Florence. It was a Greek high school. So many learned men graduated from it and became celebrated teachers, that the people said it was like the wooden horse at the siege of Troy, out of which came so many Greek warriors fully armed for the fight.

Although Lorenzo was called "The Magnificent" by the people of Florence, and was apparently so generous toward them, yet Florence was not really enriched by him. He only made it grander and more famous by his administration, but he completed that subversion of the Florentine republic for which his father and his grandfather had well prepared the way.

Florence, although so splendid, was full of corruption, her rulers violating oaths, betraying trusts, and living only for pleasure. From the days of Lorenzo de Medici her power has steadily declined.

CHAPTER 2

Christopher Columbus

(1435-1506)

ONE day in the autumn of 1486 a stranger knocked at the gate of a convent called "La Rabida," not far from the little Spanish seaport of Palos. He held by the hand a little boy, and when the monk who opened the door asked what was wanted he answered, "My child and I are tired and hungry. Will you give us a morsel of bread, and let us rest here awhile?"

They were invited to enter, and food was set before them. During the meal the stranger began to talk about the Western Ocean and what must be on the other side of it. "Most men," he said, "think that beyond the Azores there is nothing but a sea of darkness; but I believe that beyond those islands there is another and a larger land."

The prior of the convent, and the physician of Palos who happened to be present, were greatly interested in what their visitor had to say, and asked him to tell them his name and something of his history.

"I am called Christopher Columbus," he said.

"I was born in Genoa, and there my boyhood was spent. I loved when a child to watch the sailors haul up the anchor and let loose the sails when a ship began her voyage. My play was to learn the names of the ropes and find out what each was for.

"My father sent me to the University of Pavia; and there I learned about the stars that guide the seaman on his way. I also learned to draw maps and charts. While drawing those maps I used to wonder whether there was not some land beyond the Canaries and the Azores.

"At fifteen I became a sailor. I went on voyages to England and Ireland, to Greece and elsewhere. On one of my voyages our ship was wrecked on the rocky coast of Portugal, but I got to land by the help of a plank. I stayed awhile in Portugal, and there I married the daughter of a sea captain who was the governor of Porto Santo, one of the Madeira Islands.

"I afterwards visited Porto Santo, and there I met many men whose lives were spent in sailing the sea. They told me some wonderful tales. One said that a Portuguese pilot named Martin Vicente had picked up at sea, twelve hundred miles west of Portugal, a piece of strange wood that had been carved by the hand of man. My brother-in-law said that he had seen at Porto Santo great pieces of jointed canes; and that a friend had told him about two human bodies which had been washed up at Flores, 'very broad-faced' and not at all like Christians.

"All these things made me believe more firmly in the idea of a land to the westward; and at length I determined to find that land.

"But I was poor. I could not buy a ship nor pay a crew. I went to my native Genoa, where the masts in the harbor rise as close as the trees in a wood. I explained my plans to the rich merchants there, and begged them to help me. But my countrymen were afraid to send any vessel of theirs beyond the Azores. They thought that west of those islands, there was nothing but the 'Sea of Darkness.'

"I went to Lisbon and asked the Portuguese king for help. Again I was disappointed; but I was not discouraged.

"I then came to Spain, and at last the good Queen Isabella heard my story. A council of learned men was called to consider my plan. They said it was wild, and advised her Majesty to give me no aid.

"Thus, I am again disappointed. The little money that I had is spent, and I am a beggar. It seems as if the world is against me. Yet I am sure that there is a land beyond the sea."

The prior, the physician, and the monks who had gathered about Columbus were much interested. Father Perez, one of the monks, had been confessor to Queen Isabella, and he wrote a letter to her begging that she would see Columbus again. She consented, and Columbus went from the convent to the palace to see her. The queen again refused his request, and Columbus set out for France hoping that the king of that country might help him. But one of the officers of Isabella's court persuaded her to change her mind, and a messenger was sent to bring Columbus back into the royal presence.

Columbus At the Court of Ferdinand And Isabella

King Ferdinand and Queen Isabella were in camp at Santa Fe near Granada, which they had but lately captured from the floors; and there they signed an agreement to supply Columbus with two ships, and to pay the crews.

It was easy for the sovereigns to promise crews and to pay them; but it was very hard to find men who were willing to sail on such a voyage. Even the criminals who were promised pardon if they would go, refused. To sail into the "Sea of Darkness" seemed certain death to them.

At last, however, all difficulties were overcome. Two wealthy gentlemen added a third ship to the two supplied by the king and queen; and the wonderful voyage began. The Santa Maria with a crew of fifty men was commanded by Columbus himself; the Pinta with thirty men was in charge of Martin Pinzon; and the Nina or "Baby" with twenty-four men was commanded by Martin's brother, Vicente Pinzon.

At eight o'clock on the morning of August 3, 1492, the sails were hoisted, and the little expedition left the harbor of Palos.

On the third day out, the Pinta lost her rudder. Fortunately they were then not far from the Canary Islands. They therefore steered for Teneriffe where they had the vessel repaired.

When they had sailed about six weeks they were astonished to find that the magnetic needle varied from its usual direction. Soon after observing this, they reached a part of the ocean where a great field of seaweed lay all around them. This was what is called the "Sargasso Sea," and the ships of Columbus were the first that ever sailed across it.

They observed another strange thing. The wind in this part of the ocean blew steadily, night and day, to the westward. It was the northeast trade wind, which was unknown to sailors along the coast and in the inland seas.

They had excellent weather; but the men began to be fearful lest they could never beat back against the trade wind; and it was hard to keep them in good spirits.

Happily, soon afterward, they saw some birds, and that made them sure that land was not far off. Then the Pinta fished up a fragment of sugar cane and a log of wood; and the Nina sighted a green branch covered with dog-rose flowers.

At ten o'clock one night, Columbus saw a light ahead; and the next morning they landed on one of the Bahama Islands. Which island this was we are not quite sure; but it was probably the one which the natives called Guanahani. Columbus named it San Salvador.

Columbus Landing at San Salvador

When Columbus stepped from his boat he carried with him the royal banner of Spain. Kneeling upon the shore with his companions, he kissed the ground, gave thanks to God, and took possession of the land in the name of Ferdinand and Isabella.

The expedition afterwards discovered the islands of Cuba, Haiti and others of the West India group.

On the shore of Haiti the Santa Maria went aground and became a wreck. With the two remaining vessels, Columbus soon afterwards set sail for Spain, and on the 15th of March, 1493, he dropped anchor in the port of Palos.

Ferdinand and Isabella were then at Barcelona, and they received him with great honor. He showed them curious plants and gayly-colored parrots, and, more interesting than these, nine natives whom he had brought from the newly-discovered islands.

There was now no doubt that Columbus was right, and that the "Sea of Darkness" beyond the Azores was only a dream.

It was determined that Columbus should make another expedition. In six months seventeen vessels and fifteen hundred men were ready to sail, and the second great voyage was begun. It was on this voyage that Jamaica, Porto Rico, and several smaller islands were discovered.

The Reception of Columbus At Barcelona

Most of the fifteen hundred men, however, went with Columbus, not in the hope of discovering new lands, but for the purpose of colonizing the island of Haiti. Columbus had learned on his first voyage that on that island there were deposits of gold; so now a mining town was founded in the gold region of Haiti, and the work of digging was begun. But the Spaniards were not fond of work. They therefore made slaves of the natives and forced them to dig in the mines; and a large quantity of gold was secured.

Some of the greedy colonists thought of another and easier way of making money. They captured a number of the natives and sent them to Spain to be sold as slaves; and, strange to say, Columbus permitted this.

When Queen Isabella heard of it she was very angry with Columbus, and asked him who had given him the right to make slaves of her subjects. She commanded that every one of the Indians should be made free and sent home.

This enslaving of the Indians was the beginning of the downfall of Columbus. Isabella never afterwards felt toward him as she had before.

However, when he returned to Spain he related a pitiful tale about the sufferings of the colonists in Haiti; and the queen furnished him with supplies for them, and provided a fleet of six vessels with which he set sail on May 30, 1498.

On this third voyage a new land was discovered. One day, three hill-tops were seen rising out of the sea, and soon the ships approached a large island. Columbus called it, from its three peaks, Trinidad, and the island is still known by that name.

From Trinidad they sailed to the southwest until they approached another shore. Columbus had now discovered the southern grand division of the New World, but he did not know this. He supposed that the land was only another island.

He was anxious to get back to the colony on the island of Haiti, and so, sailing now to the northward, the ships in due time reached their harbor.

In Haiti there were men plotting against Columbus. Some of the colonists who had not found so much gold as they had hoped for, returned to Spain and complained to the king that Columbus was managing the colony badly.

Ferdinand and Isabella partly believed what they said. As Columbus had done one wrong thing when he made slaves of the Indians, the king and queen thought he might do wrong in other things.

Accordingly, they sent to Haiti a man named Bobadilla (bo ba deel' yd) to take charge of the colony; and Bobadilla on his arrival, accused Columbus of cruelty and injustice, and sent him to Spain in chains. The captain of the vessel in which he sailed wished to remove these fetters, but Columbus would not allow him to do so. He wore them to the end of the voyage, and kept them as relics ever afterwards.

Columbus in Chains

As soon as the vessel reached Spain, Columbus wrote a letter to the king and queen telling them what he had done, and what had been done to him. When Isabella read it, she is said to have shed tears. His fetters were at once removed; and Ferdinand and Isabella refused to listen to the charges which Bobadilla had made against him.

Columbus never so much as imagined that he had discovered a new continent. He supposed that Cuba, Jamaica, and the other islands which he visited were some of what are called the "Indies", or islands near India. For a long time everybody else supposed so too; and hence it is that Cuba and the neighboring islands have always been called the West Indies.

About this time, the Pope divided between Spain and Portugal all the newly-discovered lands, and all that might afterwards be discovered. The dividing line was a meridian passing three hundred leagues west of the Azores. Spain's share was all that lay west of this meridian, and Portugal's all that lay east of it.

Spain was jealous of Portugal, and anxious to secure a part of that kingdom's share. Columbus suggested a way to do this. He assured Ferdinand and Isabella that by sailing still farther to the westward, beyond the West Indies, it would be possible to reach some of the islands which might be claimed by Portugal; and of course he was correct in this view.

He asked the sovereigns for a fleet with which to make the attempt; and in 1502, with four ships and a hundred and fifty men, he set sail from Cadiz. On the voyage he landed at Jamaica and other islands; but although he was absent more than two years, he accomplished nothing of importance.

He returned to Spain in 1504, and died two years later.

His body was buried at Valladolid (val ya do leed'), but was afterwards carried across the ocean and interred in the cathedral of Santo Domingo on the island of Haiti. When that island was ceded by the Spaniards to France, the remains of the great navigator were removed to Havana; and there they rested until after the war between the United States and Spain, when they were taken back to Spain

CHAPTER 3

Ferdinand of Aragon

(1452-1516)

FERDINAND OF ARAGON was the son of John II, king of the Spanish provinces of Navarre and Aragon.

For centuries before Ferdinand's time Spain had been divided into a number of petty kingdoms. Some of them were in the hands of the Christians and the rest belonged to the Moors whose ancestors were partly Arabs and partly people of North Africa.

The Moors were Mohammedans. About seven hundred years before the time of Ferdinand they had crossed the Mediterranean Sea and invaded Spain, capturing nearly the whole of that country with the exception of the provinces which lay in the extreme north.

For a long time, therefore, Spain was a Mohammedan country. But the Spanish Christians became more numerous and more powerful; and during the time of the Crusades, they were almost continually at war with their Moorish neighbors.

At the time that Ferdinand was born they had regained all Spain except the one kingdom of Granada.

In Granada, several thousand Moors still lived. They irrigated the land and cultivated rice. They planted mulberry trees and were famed for their production of silk. They even grew sugar cane, and were the first to make Europeans acquainted with sugar. The beautiful city of Granada was their capital and great stronghold at the time when Ferdinand became king; and even to-day travelers go by thousands to see the remains of its splendid palaces.

The City of Granada

Ferdinand married Isabella who was the queen of Castile; so that under these two sovereigns three of the Christian kingdoms of Spain—Aragon, Navarre and Castile—were united.

It seemed to them, however, a disgrace to Christianity, as well as an injury to Spain, that there should be a Mohammedan kingdom in their country. They therefore determined to add Granada to their domains and a bitter war against the Moors was begun.

General Gonsalvo, a famous soldier, whom the Spaniards still delight to call "the great captain" was put in command of the Spanish army.

Granada was invaded. Sallies were made by the Moors; and many single combats were fought between their champions and the Christian knights. But no great battle was fought, and the war continued for months.

At one time the Spanish camp of tents took fire by accident and was destroyed. A permanent town with houses of stone was then built by Ferdinand for his army. The town still stands, and is called Santa Fe.

When the Moorish king, who was named Boabdil (bo ab' deel), heard that King Ferdinand had threatened to take Granada, he laughed in scorn; nevertheless, he at once made ready to defend his city.

The war lasted more than ten years. The Moors defended themselves bravely; but the Spaniards devastated the fruitful lands of their country, totally destroyed twenty-four of their principal towns, and then besieged the city of Granada itself. The Moors held out bravely for almost a year; then, being on the verge of starvation, they surrendered Granada.

Lion Court of the Alhambra, Granada

Boabdil Surrenders

It was agreed that Boabdil should reign over a small territory, and should do homage to Ferdinand for it. He soon grew tired of his little kingdom, however, and crossed the Mediterranean to Africa, where, not long afterwards, he perished in battle. He was the last of the Moorish kings of Spain.

The year 1492 proved to be a memorable one for Ferdinand and Isabella, and for the country which they governed. It began with the conquest of Granada; and it ended in seeing Spain's condition wonderfully improved in almost every particular. For two hundred years the Turks had been the terror of Christendom. Christians who traded with India were obliged to sail across the Mediterranean Sea, and to pass through lands that belonged to the Turks to reach that country. They had also to bring back through those lands and across the Mediterranean whatever goods they bought in India.

Their ships and cargoes were often captured by Turkish pirates, and the owners and crews were made slaves. Thousands of such Christian slaves were chained to the rowing benches of the Turkish galleys and were cruelly whipped if they did not obey their masters. The people of those times wished to find a way by which to reach India without encountering these difficulties and dangers.

More than once did the different nations of Europe join together to make war against the Turks. Ferdinand himself, after taking Granada from the Moors, sent a fleet across the Mediterranean and captured Algiers, the great stronghold of the Turkish pirates.

After a Moorish Victory

Many Italian, Spanish and Portuguese Christians who had been slaves for years came home, most of them sick, and all of them poor. You can imagine how the sight of them, when they landed, made the people wish for some safer way to India. When, therefore, Columbus offered to find one, Ferdinand and Isabella supplied him with money and ships and men.

He did not, indeed, find a new way to India, but he thought he had done so, and so did the king and queen. The people of Spain, and of Europe generally, rejoiced at the thought that trade with India could in future be carried on without so great a loss of life and treasure.

While Columbus failed in this one important point, his discoveries were of great value to Spain, for they gave her immense possessions in the "new world" and added largely to her wealth and power.

Ferdinand was at first rather cold toward Columbus. He did not have much faith either in the great discoverer or in his plans. The real credit of Spain's assistance belongs far more to Queen Isabella than to King Ferdinand. But by consolidating and strengthening his dominions, Ferdinand lifted Spain into a prominent position among the European nations; and his influence was felt for many years after his death, which occurred in 1516.

CHAPTER 4

Vasco Da Gama

(1469-1524)

ONE day in the year 1497 King Manuel of Portugal was at work in his study. It was five years since Columbus had brought the news to Ferdinand of Aragon that a way to the Indies had been discovered by sailing westward; for Columbus, as we have learned, supposed that the islands on which he had landed were some of the East India islands. Manuel was busy planning an expedition which he hoped might discover a passage to the Indies by sailing eastward.

A nobleman entered the room where he was sitting. "Vasco da Gama," said the king when he saw him, "I make you captain of my expedition. Take any one of the ships you please, and let your brother command another. If it please God, you will discover India."

Three ships, not larger than the schooners which sail up and down our rivers, were lying at anchor in the harbor of Lisbon. They were named after the three archangels, Michael, Gabriel, and Raphael. They were laden with everything which the king and Vasco thought might be useful on a voyage of discovery, and among the men who were to sail in them were carpenters, blacksmiths, rope makers, and such other skilled workmen as were likely to be of service.

When the vessels were ready to start, a solemn service was held in the great cathedral of Lisbon. All who were going on the expedition were there. The king and queen were also present; and when the bishop had pronounced the blessing, the king presented to Vasco da Gama the royal standard. "Let it fly," he said, "at the masthead of your ship."

From the cathedral, Vasco and his men marched to the harbor. The ships were decorated with flags, and the king's standard was run up at the masthead of the one which Vasco was to command. Guns were fired, the anchors were heaved, the sails were loosed, and the little fleet floated down to the mouth of the river.

There in the port of Belem they waited three days for a fair wind, and then the voyage began. A Portuguese writer says, "So many tears were shed when they were sailing away that the shore may well be named the shore of tears;" and Camoens, the great poet of Portugal wrote,

> *Uncounted as the grains of golden sand,*
> *The tears of thousands fell on Belem's strand.*

The ships were so long sailing down the coast of Africa that the sailors became discouraged. They insisted that the land must extend entirely across the sea, and that it had no end.

Vasco da Gama knew that it had an end; for another great navigator, named Bartholomew Diaz, had already found the end and called it the "Cape of Storms," because of the very bad weather he had encountered there.

Near this cape Vasco also met with storms, and his men wished to turn back. But, like Columbus, Vasco was determined to go on. Some of the men formed a conspiracy to kill him, and he was obliged to put the mutineers in irons. At length, they doubled the cape, sailed to the north-eastward, and left the storms behind them.

The ships had been greatly damaged by the winds and waves. They were leaking badly, and the sailors had to work at the pumps night and day. Wearied and disheartened they again requested that the voyage might be given up, and that they might be allowed to return to their homes.

Vasco saw that the ships must be repaired, and, besides this, all were in need of water. He therefore steered toward the land and kept a sharp lookout for a safe harbor. If you look at the map of Africa, you will see that part of the southeast coast is called Natal. (na tal'). This is the Portuguese name for Christmas Day. Vasco named this part of the coast Natal because he sailed past it on that day.

Farther on, the voyagers were delighted to see the mouth of a river. Steering into it, and sailing some distance up the stream, they found a place where they could land. There they stayed some time and repaired their ships. One, however, was so battered and broken that she could not be made seaworthy; they therefore took her to pieces and used the wood to repair the other two.

Vasco named this stream the "River of Mercy."

One day some of the natives came to visit them. The sailors offered them slices of bread with marmalade; but their visitors did not taste a morsel until they saw the Portuguese eating. When they had once tasted, it seemed as though they would never have enough.

Da Gama showed them a looking-glass, a thing they had never seen before. They were greatly amused, and laughed loudly when they saw their faces reflected in it. Sailing from the River of Mercy, Vasco steered northward, keeping always in sight of land. After some days he saw a ship at anchor and at once sent a boat to find out where he was. But the native sailors were afraid, and jumping into a canoe paddled away as fast as they could.

The Portuguese boat soon overtook them, and then all but one of the natives threw themselves into the sea and swam to shore. The one man remaining in the canoe could not swim, and so the Portuguese took him on board one of their ships. He proved to be a Moor, and as he was able to act as an interpreter, he became very useful to them.

Not long after this another vessel was seen. She was under full sail, but Vasco's ship soon came up with her. Two negroes on board the strange vessel spoke a language that some of the negroes on the ships of the Portuguese understood; and from them they learned that she was on her way to a harbor of India called Cambay. This was good news to da Gama, and they followed her into an African harbor called Mozambique (mo zam beek').

It was now nearly a year since they had sailed from Lisbon; and all were delighted to enter a port where they could see houses and people.

Soon after they came to anchor, the sheik or governor of the city of Mozambique paid them a visit. He came upon two canoes lashed together, poles and planks being placed upon them to make a floor, above which was stretched a large piece of matting. Under the matting sat the sheik and ten companions. The sheik wore a jacket of velvet; a blue cloth embroidered with threads of gold was wrapped round his body; and a silken sash was tied round his waist. A dagger was stuck in his sash, and he carried a sword in his hand.

When he reached the ships trumpets were sounded, and Vasco and his officers greeted him with the heartiest welcome. The Moor interpreted everything that they said, or that the Portuguese said to them.

The Conspiracy

The sheik asked the Portuguese of what merchandise they were in search. Thereupon they showed him some pepper, cinnamon and ginger. He then promised to send pilots who would steer their vessels to India; and after he left the ships two men came on board who said they had been sent for that purpose.

Before the Portuguese were ready to resume their voyage, the sheik invited Vasco to dine with him, and advised that all the sick men should be sent on shore.

Vasco learned from his Moor that this was a trick to get them into the sheik's power, and so he declined the invitation.

A boat was sent to get fresh water, and one of the sheik's pilots went to show the Portuguese where the spring was. He said that midnight was the only time at which they could row to the spring because of the tide. But from midnight until morning he kept them rowing about from place to place, and no water was found.

Seeing at length that the Portuguese were growing angry, he jumped overboard and swam a long distance under water, not rising till he was far away from the boat. In this way he escaped.

Vasco now sailed away, but he put the other pilot in irons. He could not trust him; for the Moor had found out that the sheik had ordered both the pilots to steer the ships upon the shoals and wreck them.

The next harbor Vasco reached was Mombasa (Mom bas' a). The sheik of Mozambique had sent word to the king, who was a friend of his, that two ships would soon arrive at Mombasa whose captains were great robbers—that they meant to bring a large fleet and take possession of Mombasa and Mozambique; and that the wisest thing to do was to make prisoners of the strangers and put them to death.

As soon as the king of Mombasa learned that the two ships had actually arrived outside the harbor he sent a kind message to Vasco, inviting him to land and make a treaty. He sent two pilots to take the vessels into the harbor because there were dangerous shoals at its entrance. He also sent a large boat loaded with sheep, sugar cane, citrons, lemons and oranges, as a present.

The sick men were delighted with the fruit. Vasco sent two men on shore to buy some other things that were needed; but the king said they might have whatever they wished without paying.

A guide was given to them who took them all over the city, and particularly to a part where, he said, Christians lived. The people there pretended to be

Christians but were not. They treated the Portuguese kindly, and begged them to stop all night at their houses.

This kindness was only pretended. The truth was that the king had given orders to the pilots to run Vasco's vessels on the shoals of the harbor, and they tried to do it. Vasco's ship, however, did not obey the helm when they were turning to enter the harbor; but it went so close to the shoal, that the officer in command ordered the sailors to let go the anchor and haul down the sails. In a moment this was done, and the other ship did the same. The two pilots, thinking their plans were discovered, jumped into the water and swam to a boat and escaped.

Vasco determined to leave these treacherous people at once, but his anchor had become fixed so firmly in the rocks of the shoal that the crew could not raise it. They labored at this all night, and the cable parting in the morning, they had to leave the anchor and sail away without it.

The next port that they reached was Melinda. Here they were treated with real kindness; for a soothsayer, whom the king trusted, told him that the Portuguese would someday be lords of India, and that he had better make a treaty with them.

The king therefore invited Vasco and his brother to land and settle upon the terms of a treaty. The Portuguese, however, were distrustful. They proposed that the king and they should have their talk sitting in boats near the shore, and to this the king agreed. Vasco and his brother dressed themselves in their handsomest suits and went in their boats seated on chairs that were covered with crimson velvet. Each of the boats carried two small guns which were fired as a salute, and then the crews rowed toward the shore.

The king now came on board one of the boats, and sat on a seat prepared for him. He said that he wished to be always friendly with the king of Portugal. Vasco da Gama and his brother knelt to kiss the king's hand, but he made them rise. Then the trumpets sounded and the ships fired all their guns.

Vasco presented to the king a splendid sword in a case of gold, saying, "Sire, we give you this sword in the name of our king and promise to maintain peace and friendship with you forever." The king answered "I promise and swear by my religion to keep peace and friendship forever with my new brother the king of Portugal." Thousands of the king's people were gathered on the shore and witnessed all this.

After the treaty had been made Vasco wished at once to sail to India. But he had to cross the great Indian Ocean, and favorable winds would not blow until August, and it was now only May. So for three months the Portuguese remained at Melinda.

Vasco De Gama in Calicut

Just before they sailed Vasco erected, on a hill near the city, a white marble column on which was inscribed the name of King Manuel.

As a parting gift the king of Melinda sent to the Portuguese a large boatload of rice, butter, sugar, cocoanuts, sheep, fowls and vegetables.

Sailing eastward now for about twenty days Vasco at length sighted land. It was the shore of Calicut, a city in India. The vessels were soon anchored in the harbor.

Thus, the great sea route to the land of silks and spices had been discovered. A factory, or trading house, was established at Calicut, and for the next hundred years little Portugal was the sovereign of the eastern seas, and the greatest commercial nation of Europe.

Da Gama died in 1524. The Portuguese honor him as we honor Columbus; and Camoens made him the hero of his "Lusiad," the greatest poem in the Portuguese language.

CHAPTER 5

Chevalier Bayard

(1476-1524)

ONE of the greatest heroes of France in the sixteenth century, was the Chevalier Bayard, or, as we may translate his title, Bayard the Knight. His real name was Pierre du Terrail; and he came of a famous family of warriors who had done excellent service for their country. He was born in the year 1476, at Bayard Castle, near the town of Grenoble, in France; and it was from the family estate that he took the name of Bayard.

He is often called "the knight without fear and without reproach." He was so brave that he never feared a foe; so good that no one ever reproached him for doing wrong. His father and grandfather were warriors, and no other life than that of a soldier was thought of for young Pierre.

The first step in the education of a knight was to become a page. When fourteen years old Pierre began his military training as a page to a famous warrior of that time, Duke Charles of Savoy.

Mounted upon a pony, and dressed in a suit of silk and velvet, he was a handsome little fellow; but, better than that, he was courteous and obliging. The pages carried messages from the duke and duchess to their friends; and Pierre was such a faithful messenger that he became a general favorite.

He had not been a year at the ducal palace when the duke had to make a visit to his sovereign, King Charles VIII of France. He thought that he could do no better service to the king than to offer him his bright little page.

The king was charmed with him, and for three years Pierre was page to the king. He was then promoted to the rank of gentleman. He was only seventeen years old; but it was not long before he became famous, and everybody at the court was speaking in his praise.

It was the fashion, in those days, for brave men to show their skill as soldiers by fighting with one another in "tournaments" or sham fights. A lady, chosen for the occasion and called the Queen of Beauty, presented prizes to the victors. The knights who wished to fight hung their shields on the boughs of trees near the tournament grounds as a challenge. Whoever wished to accept the challenge struck the hanging shield with his lance or sword.

Tournament

A tournament was to be held in honor of King Charles and the ladies of his court; and Sir Claude de Vaudre (vo' dray), who was the champion of France, hung up his shield. Among those who struck it was young Pierre; and when the tournament was held, he won the prize. He had vanquished Sir Claude.

Not long after this, he held a tournament himself, and was the challenger. Forty-eight warriors struck the shield that he hung up; and one by one they were defeated by him in the tournament.

But it was real war for which the young soldier longed, and very soon it came. The French king invaded Italy, and the Italian states formed a league against him. In a battle which was fought, although the Italians were more than five times as numerous as the French, King Charles won the day.

The champion of the fight was Bayard. Two horses were killed under him, his sword was hacked, and his coat of mail was battered; but in spite of all, he captured the royal standard of Naples. He was brought before the sovereign holding this trophy in his hand; and then and there, on the battlefield, the king made him a knight. Charles soon afterwards died, but under the new king, Louis VII, the French again fought in Italy. Marching across the Alps, they captured the province of Milan and held it; but the city of Milan was won back from them by the Italian Prince Sforza.

Three hundred of Sforza's horsemen were one day encamped near the city, when Bayard, with only fifty comrades, made an assault on them. The fight was wild, but at length the Italians fled and galloped swiftly through the gates into Milan.

Bayard, supposing that his comrades were close behind him, dashed after the flying Italians into the great square of the city. A fierce attack was now made on him, while he on his part slashed right and left with his battle-axe, killing or wounding many of his assailants. At length however he was overpowered, and taken prisoner. The din of this conflict was heard by Sforza, and he ordered the knight to be brought before him. When Sforza had heard his story, he said, "Lord Bayard, I set you free. I ask no ransom. I will grant whatever favor you ask."

"Prince," replied Bayard, "I thank you. I ask but my horse and my armor."

Then bidding his generous foe adieu, the knight rode out of the city, and soon reached the camp of his friends.

Sometime after this there was war between France and Spain. Both claimed certain parts of Italy, and so the fighting was done on Italian soil.

Once the French and Spanish were on opposite sides of the river. There was a bridge between them which the French held and could easily defend.

The Spanish commander knew of a ford some distance down the stream. He proposed to draw the French away from the bridge, so that his men might capture it.

Accordingly, taking a body of troops, he went to the ford, as if he were intending to cross it. The French, on seeing him move, abandoned their post at the bridge and marched toward the ford.

The bridge being thus left undefended, a body of two hundred Spaniards suddenly appeared and marched directly toward it. Bayard saw that not a moment was to be lost. Putting on his armor, he leaped to the saddle, and spurring his horse, was on the bridge before the Spaniards could reach it.

The Spaniards quickly arrived; but Bayard stood upon the defensive and, swinging his heavy broadsword, he slew an enemy with every blow. The Spaniards thought him some demon, and checked their furious charge. Meanwhile, a band of French horsemen rushed like a whirlwind to the bridge, and drove the Spaniards back to the farther side.

After this exploit men said of Bayard, "Single, he has the might of an army."

Once, at the siege of a castle, he was crossing the ramparts at the head of a storming party, when he received his first wound. He was struck by a pike, and the sharp-pointed head remained fixed in his thigh.

He was taken to a house nearby, where a mother and her daughters had shut themselves in in dread of their lives. The mother timidly opened the door, and the wounded knight was taken in; and there for six long weeks he lay, and was nursed as carefully as if he had been a member of the family. And he on his part was their protection, for a band of his soldiers guarded the house until all danger was past.

On the day of Bayard's departure, the mother begged him to accept a little steel box as a remembrance. It contained twenty-five hundred ducats in gold, which would be more than a thousand dollars of our money.

"Give five hundred for me," said Bayard, "to the nuns whose convent near your house has been pillaged; and as for the rest, young ladies, I beg you each to accept a thousand ducats from me; for I owe you much for your care."

War was still raging in North Italy. Francis I had become sovereign of France; and like the king who reigned before him claimed part of Italy for his domain.

The French army lay encamped about the town of Marignano (ma reen ya no). The king was about to take his supper, when suddenly the enemy marched in full force from the gates and assaulted his camp. The French were instantly in arms, and the battle raged as long as there was light to see a foe. Both armies lay under arms all night, and before the sun rose, the fighting had begun again.

The contest has been called the "Battle of the Giants." The French performed marvelous exploits and won the day, but Bayard outshone all his comrades still.

The evening after the victory, King Francis knighted many brave men on the field of battle. But a wonderful honor was chosen for Bayard. The king made proclamation that he himself would receive the rank of knight from his champion.

Bayard Defending the Bridge

Accordingly he knelt before the Chevalier, and Bayard, striking the shoulder of Francis with his sword, said, "Rise, Sir Francis;" and thus gave him knighthood.

When, in 1520, Francis I met Henry VIII of England near Calais upon the celebrated "Field of the Cloth of Gold," the knights of both countries vied with each other in what were, perhaps, the grandest tournaments ever held; and Bayard again won the greatest renown.

It had always been the Knight's wish that he might die in battle. And so he did.

In 1524 he was fighting under the French commander, Lord Bonnivet. Want of supplies and sickness compelled Bonnivet to retreat. The Spaniards placed men in ambush along the road which the French had to take. From one of these hidden foes the chevalier received his death wound. A comrade helped him from his horse, and laid him under the shadow of a tree.

Bayard felt that he was dying. He charged his friend to turn his face toward the foe, and then to care for his own safety. When the Spaniards reached the spot, they found him still breathing.

The Spanish general, Lord Pescara, showed him every care, and a priest was brought to console him in his last moments. And thus, loved by friends and admired by foes, the "knight without fear and without reproach" ended his wonderful life.

CHAPTER 6

Cardinal Wolsey

(1471-1530)

NOT far from London is an old palace called Hampton Court. Had you been standing near its gateway on a Sunday about four hundred years ago, you might have heard the cry, "Make way for my Lord's Grace."

Looking toward the palace you would have seen a curious procession leaving the doorway. You would have noticed one gentleman carrying a scarlet hat; two very tall and handsome persons each carrying a silver cross; another carrying a mace, which is a wooden staff with a spiked metal ball for its head; and still another carrying the great seal of England.

After these you would have seen a number of gentlemen who made the cry which you heard. Following these was the most important person of all—a high officer of church and state, mounted on a mule which had trappings of crimson velvet and gilt stirrups. This was "my Lord's Grace." His name was Thomas Wolsey; and when people were told to make way for him, he was setting out to pay his Sunday call upon the king of England.

The red hat showed that he was a cardinal. He was also the Pope's legate, or the representative of the Pope in England. The mace, and the great seal, showed that he was Lord Chancellor of the kingdom.

Wolsey was second only to the sovereign in the kingdom—second only to the Pope in the church.

He was not born to all this greatness. His father was a butcher who lived in the town of Ipswich, in England, and in addition to his business as a butcher, kept sheep and sold wool. He was a prosperous man—neither rich nor poor.

Thomas was born in the year 1471. He was sent to the grammar school in his native town; and when only eleven was ready for college. He graduated at fifteen—so young that at college he was called the "Boy Bachelor."

One thing that made him great was that he was very clever and very industrious. He learned his lessons so well and so quickly that all his teachers were astonished.

He made up his mind after graduating to become a priest and was ordained. Then he was put in charge of a church called Limington.

Sometime after he began preaching in Limington, King Henry VII wished to marry a certain Spanish princess, and had to obtain the consent of the emperor of Germany. He needed some very wise and trusty messenger to send to Europe to arrange with the emperor about this marriage.

Bishop Fisher and other good friends of Wolsey told the king that no better man than Wolsey could be found in all England. So the young priest was invited to a conference with the king, and Henry told Wolsey what he wished him to say to the emperor. After this Wolsey hastened to Dover and embarked upon a vessel which was waiting for him.

Fair winds soon wafted Wolsey's ship across the English Channel, and swift post horses brought him to the town where the emperor was staying. The king's message was delivered and everything was arranged as Henry had desired. Wolsey then sailed back to England.

He took post horses and reached the palace by night. Next morning the king saw him, and asked why he had not yet started on his journey. He had not been away a whole week; and the king could scarcely believe that he had gone to see the emperor and had returned. Henry was greatly pleased, and put the swift and sure messenger into a much better position in the church than he already held.

After the death of Henry VII, his son Henry VIII found Wolsey a most useful person. The young king was fond of amusement, but not at all fond of business. Wolsey liked to manage the business of the kingdom.

Henry saw that Wolsey could do this, and save him a great deal of trouble; and for this reason the king made him Lord Chancellor of England. Wolsey was now for a time the real ruler of the kingdom.

Wolsey thought it wise to live in a great deal of show. He saw that it pleased the people and the king.

He built for his home the palace called Hampton Court. It was very handsome and the king greatly admired it. So, after living in it about ten years,

Wolsey gave it to his majesty as a present; and to this day it belongs to the sovereign of England.

Twice Wolsey was sent by Henry VIII with messages to Charles V; and when he traveled on state business he seemed as grand as the king himself.

The Parliament met in a large building called Westminster Hall. Wolsey used to go there from Hampton Court in great pomp, just as when he went to visit the king.

Several times every year the king went to visit the great cardinal. Then the most expensive luxuries that could be bought were served at the table. There was music and dancing. The finest singers of England were employed; and the king and the lords and ladies of the court often took part in the festivities.

But there was something more serious in Wolsey's life than the love of luxury and merrymaking. He wanted to found a college at Oxford, as other great churchmen had done, but the means were not at hand. He had received from the king the revenues of the abbey of St. Albans, and he applied to the Pope for permission to suppress a monastery at Oxford and apply its property to the new college. As the need for a new college was said to be most pressing, and as the monastery was well adapted for a house of learning the Pope consented.

Still there was not money enough for Wolsey's purpose. So he wrote to the Pope that there were many monasteries in which the monks were so few that they could not perform their office properly. Then the Pope gave to Wolsey increased powers to suppress monasteries wherever he might deem it necessary, provided the king and the founders did not object, and the monks were admitted to other monasteries. Wolsey received the king's approval and began his work.

He met with strenuous objections from the people, however, and in some places there was a riot when Wolsey's agents attempted to expel the occupants of the monasteries.

Nevertheless, the means were secured, and Christchurch College was founded, as well as a school at Ipswich.

Wolsey was a very ambitious man. He got for himself the highest positions in England; and he hoped sometime to be made pope.

He was the favorite of the king for many years; but Henry was a fickle man. If a man or woman did not do exactly as he wished, his love soon changed to hate.

Henry was married to Catherine of Aragon, the widow of his brother Arthur, the daughter of Ferdinand and Isabella, and aunt of the emperor Charles V.

Nevertheless, he fell in love with another woman named Anne Boleyn, and wished Wolsey to persuade the Pope to annul the marriage with Catherine.

Henry said he feared his marriage was illegal, and Wolsey tried to get the Pope to do what Henry and Wolsey wished. After considerable delay, for the Pope was then a prisoner, a cardinal was sent to form with Wolsey a court to try the case.

Hampton Court

Catherine was called before the court, but as Wolsey was her subject, she would not recognize the authority of the court, and appealed to Rome.

No decision was made for a long time, and Henry began to consider his case hopeless when he learned that a shrewd young man named Cranmer had said that the King ought to get opinions about his marriage from the universities.

That speech was the making of Cranmer. Henry followed his advice. No foreign university, however, would give an opinion, but pressure was brought on the English universities and a favorable answer was rendered. The women of Oxford, however, stoned the king's messengers when they came for the formal documents.

The answer of the professors was just what Henry wanted. They said he ought never to have married Catherine; and that it was right for him to marry Anne. The king was overjoyed. Catherine was divorced and Anne became the queen.

Henry thought Cranmer ought to be handsomely rewarded for helping him out of his difficulty, and so he made him archbishop of Canterbury.

Anne Boleyn thought that Wolsey was to blame for the delay in having Henry's marriage annulled and she became the bitter enemy of the cardinal. Then the king grew cold, and was easily persuaded that Wolsey had broken one of the laws of the land in having directly sent to him the Pope's "bulls."

Wolsey And Queen Catherine

There is a law in England that the Pope's bulls shall not be published unless the king allows it. But Henry himself, as he well knew, had allowed the bulls sent to Wolsey to be published. So the great cardinal had done nothing wrong against the laws of the land. However, Henry took from him the honors he had previously bestowed upon him, and ordered him to give up the great seal.

Wolsey was soon afterwards accused of high treason, and the king ordered that he should be tried. He was in a distant town at the time, and a guard of twenty-five men was sent to take him to the Tower of London.

WOLSEY AT LEICESTER

At that time Wolsey was very sick, but he rode several days with his guard toward London. When he reached the Abbey of Leicester and the abbot came out to meet him, Wolsey said to him, "Father Abbot, I have come to leave my bones with you;" and so indeed he did. He went at once to his bed and never left it.

As he was talking to Sir William Kingston, the chief of the guard, a little while before he died, he said, "If I had served God as diligently as I have served the king, he would not have given me over in my gray hairs."

The next morning, as the abbey clock was striking eight, he passed away.

He was the greatest English statesman of the age of Henry VIII.

After Wolsey's death Henry married Anne Boleyn; and he and the Parliament did just what Wolsey had foretold. They declared the Church of England independent of the Church of Rome.

CHAPTER 7

Charles V of Germany

(1500-1558)

IN 1500, eight years after the discovery of America by Columbus, a Spanish prince was born in the city of Ghent in the Netherlands. He was named Charles.

He was the grandson of Ferdinand and Isabella, and from them at the age of sixteen, he inherited the crown of Spain and the two Americas. From his father he inherited the kingdom of Naples and the Netherlands.

When he was about nineteen years old, his other grandfather the emperor of Germany died. Three great kings were then reigning Francis I, in France, Henry VIII, in England, and the young king Charles—and each of them wished to be chosen as the next emperor.

Charles was elected; and as he was the fifth German emperor who was so named, he assumed the title of Charles V.

With Germany thus added to his already vast domains, he was now the ruler of an empire greater than that of Charlemagne—greater even than that of Imperial Rome.

It is wonderful that Charles was able to attend to the affairs of countries separated from one another by such great distances. This was far more difficult then than it would be now; because at that time there were neither railroads nor steamships, neither telegraphs nor telephones. Carriage roads were few and most of them were bad. Yet Charles attended well to every part of his vast empire. Although he could not be present everywhere, his power was felt everywhere.

In 1518 Mexico was discovered by a Spaniard. An expedition was at once sent out from Cuba to take possession of the country. Ten vessels, carrying about seven hundred Spaniards, sailed under the command of Hernando Cortes. The noise of the Spanish guns and cannon made the Mexicans think that the Spaniards were gods, and could not be killed or even wounded.

The people of Tlascala (tlas ca' la) were enemies of Montezuma (mon te zoo' ma) king of Mexico; and Cortes persuaded them to join his forces. So the native and Spanish soldiers marched together to the city of Mexico.

Cortez in Battle

Montezuma thought at first that Cortes was an ancient god of the Mexicans who had once been their king, and received him with great kindness. But Cortes made the king his prisoner and kept him closely guarded. Cortes also compelled him to give the Spaniards about half a million dollars in gold.

The Mexicans were very angry with Montezuma for giving up so much treasure, and some of them revolted. Montezuma tried to pacify them with kind words; but the rebels hurled stones at him and he was severely wounded and died soon afterwards as the result of his injuries.

Cortes at length succeeded in taking possession of the city of Mexico, and the whole country thus became a part of the great empire of Charles V.

One of Charles's neighbors was exceedingly jealous of him. This was Francis I, king of France. He laid claim to the province of Navarre, in Spain, and this brought on several wars between Francis and Charles which lasted through many years.

Francis was a brave enemy. Like Hannibal he crossed the snow-covered Alps and invaded Italy. But Charles was more than a match for him. In one battle he took Francis prisoner—in another he captured the Pope—and having taken possession of Rome he kept His Holiness a prisoner in the castle of St. Angelo which belonged to the Pope himself.

Francis was at last obliged to content himself with his own kingdom; and to leave Navarre in the hands of Charles.

One of the greatest difficulties which Charles had to deal with was the religious quarrel which was going on all over Germany.

The German Empire at that time consisted of a great many separate states, such as Saxony, Bavaria and others. The rulers of these states had different titles. Some were called dukes, some princes, and some kings.

Charles V at The Siege of Metz

The rulers and people of the German states were divided into two great parties—the Roman Catholics, and the Lutherans or Protestants. The quarrel between them began about the time that Charles was born, and lasted for more than a hundred years. It was ended only by the terrible battles of the "Thirty Years' War," which came to a close in 1648.

Charles was very anxious to put a stop to the evils which arose from this quarrel. It seemed to him that the simplest way of doing so was to get rid of the Protestants altogether. But so many of the princes and people of Germany had become Protestants that he found it impossible to do this; and he was obliged to allow northern Germany to remain for the most part Protestant.

While Charles was thus trying to make the great religious parties of Germany live in peace, a new difficulty arose.

Solyman the Sublime then ruled the great empire of Turkey; and, like Francis I, he was very anxious to get possession of a slice of Charles's domains.

In 1529 he raised an immense army and laid siege to Vienna, which was then the capital of the German empire. He was defeated and beaten back. This did not, however, altogether discourage him; but with a large army, he marched into southeastern Germany.

Charles then saw his opportunity to bring together the Catholic and Protestant Germans. He called upon them to unite for the defense of the empire against the common foe. All Germany at once responded; and one of the finest armies was assembled that Europe had ever seen.

Charles took command in person and marched against the Turks. When Solyman learned of this he retreated without a battle. He saw that the wisest thing for him to do was to leave Germany in possession of the Germans, and to look more closely after his own affairs.

The Turks still continued to be troublesome, however, both on land and at sea. Solyman employed a famous pirate named Barbarossa to attack all Christian merchant vessels that ventured to sail upon the Mediterranean. Barbarossa and his master were determined that none but Turkish ships should sail that sea without paying toll to the Turks. The pirates captured the vessels of the Christians, took possession of the cargoes, and made slaves of all whom they found on board.

Charles made up his mind to put a stop to all this. He therefore attacked Tunis, on the northern shore of Africa, which was Barbarossa's stronghold. Barbarossa was defeated, Tunis was captured, and thousands of Christian slaves were set free.

This caused great rejoicing all over Europe; and Charles was regarded as a benefactor of Christian seafaring people.

All these wars cost a great deal of money; and some of Charles's subjects made strong objections to paying the taxes levied upon them.

The Dutch people, in particular, complained bitterly. The people of Ghent, the very town in which Charles was born, positively refused to pay. They felt very much as our ancestors did who fought in the Revolutionary War. They thought that people who paid taxes should have something to say about the way in which the taxes should be spent.

Charles considered that it was not only the duty of the people to pay, but that it was his sole right to decide what should be done with the money. He therefore determined to punish the people of Ghent.

He took away the charter which gave the citizens the right to choose their own magistrates, and he appointed officers of his own choosing to manage their affairs. He also caused those persons who had advised the people not to pay to be treated as traitors and to be put to death.

In an attempt to take Algiers, in 1541, his fleet was wrecked and more than half his army perished; and although this was a favorite object with Charles the project had to be abandoned.

As he grew older, Charles found that it was quite impossible to manage his vast empire just as he wished to do. The pirates of Algiers still went on robbing, and more than half of his people in Germany would be Protestants in spite of all that he could say or do.

He was greatly discouraged; and, in 1554, he gave the Netherlands and the kingdom of Naples to his son Philip.

He then called together the "States General," or Congress of the Netherlands, at Brussels; and with his right hand resting upon a crutch, and his left upon the shoulder of the young Prince of Orange, he made a very solemn address.

He said that his infirmities made it necessary for him to give up the cares of government. He then asked the "States General" to forgive whatever errors he had committed during his reign, and to accept Philip as his successor.

The whole assembly burst into tears and sobs; and Charles himself, completely overcome, sank into a chair and wept like a child.

Two years after this he resigned the crown of Spain; and, after two years more, gave up his position as emperor of Germany.

He caused a palace to be built near the monastery of Yuste (yoos' tay), in Spain; and there he spent the last days of his life.

The story is told that he amused himself with trying to make a number of clocks in different rooms of the palace keep the same time. Finding that he could not do this, he is said to have remarked that it was no wonder he could not make all the people in his kingdom live and act as he desired.

Charles V at Yuste

Although extremely ambitious and overbearing he managed to maintain a strong hold on his people; and some of the events of his career exercised a powerful influence upon the later history of Europe.

During his days of retirement he was very fond of attending the religious services of the monastery, and of listening to the reports of messengers who came to tell him the news from all parts of his former domain. His strength rapidly failed; and he died in 1558.

CHAPTER 8

Solyman the Sublime

(1490–1566)

SOLYMAN I (sol' e man), sometimes called the Sublime, was sultan of Turkey when Charles V was emperor of Germany. He was born about the year 1490, and became sultan at the age of twenty-five.

When his father, Selim I, lay upon his death bed, he said to his son Solyman, "My son, I am passing away, and you will soon be ruler of Turkey. During my reign I have tried to make my empire a strong military power. Promise me that you will carry on the work which I have begun. Try to make the Turkish nation respected and feared."

"Father," said Solyman, "I will do all that I can to make my country the equal of any in the world."

We know nothing of the Turks until about the time of Louis IX, the crusading king of France. Then a small body of the strange warlike people came from central Asia; and in about fifty years they had gained possession of all that part of Asia which we call Asia Minor.

Only the narrow strait called the Bosporus, about one mile wide, lay between them and the beautiful city of Constantinople, which was then the capital of the Eastern Roman Empire. From the Asiatic side of the Bosporus the Turks could see the palaces of the Christian city and the church of Santa Sophia (so fee' a), then the most magnificent church in Christendom.

In 1453, when Gutenberg was printing his first Latin Bible, the Turks attacked Constantinople with a powerful fleet. The Greeks had put a chain across the mouth of the harbor, but the Turks made a plank road five miles long, drew their war galleys over it, and launched them under the very walls of the city. Their cannon made a breach in the walls, and through it the Turks entered and stormed the place.

The Greek emperor, though fighting bravely, fell; and the Turks completely overpowered the Christians.

Constantinople

At sunset the sultan gave thanks for his victory. The church of St. Sophia was at once turned into a mosque, and so remains to the present day.

By the capture of Constantinople the Turks gained their first foothold in Europe; and for more than two hundred years afterward it was their constant effort to make themselves masters of the whole continent.

With this idea in mind, Solyman invaded Servia and besieged Belgrade, the capital. Belgrade was at that time one of the strongest fortifications in the world. It was also the great stronghold of the Christians of the east. Solyman captured the city and annexed Servia to the empire of Turkey.

He next invaded Hungary, and in 1526 a terrible battle was fought at Mohacs (mo hach'). Solyman gained the victory. A great number of the Hungarian nobility perished and their king, Louis II, lost his life.

A large part of the valley of the Danube was now at the mercy of Solyman, and portions of it continued to be Turkish territory for three centuries.

Triumphal Entry of The Turks

The Turkish Invasion

After this battle some of the Hungarian nobles elected as king a man named John Zapolya (za' pol ya). A prince who had a better right to the throne was Ferdinand, duke of Austria, who was the brother of Charles V.

Zapolya could not drive Ferdinand's troops out of the kingdom. He asked Solyman to help him. This Solyman was glad to do because he saw that it might give him the opportunity to take possession of all Hungary. With a large army he marched into the country. He took from Ferdinand the fortified city of Buda and made it his own headquarters.

Not long afterwards he appeared with an army of nearly two hundred thousand men before Vienna which was Ferdinand's capital. After trying several times to storm the city, however, he had to abandon the siege. But fighting continued until it was agreed that Zapolya should be king of one half of Hungary, and of course he became a vassal to Solyman.

Sometime later Solyman compelled Ferdinand to pay tribute for the other half—thus all Hungary became a province of the Turkish empire, and this it continued to be for more than a hundred and fifty years.

All of northern Africa was Mohammedan, and from its shores it was easy to send out expeditions to attack the ships of Christian nations. Solyman selected Tunis as the headquarters for his fleet. His great admiral, Barbarossa, was the terror of every Christian seaman. He forced the nations who carried on commerce on the Mediterranean to pay him tribute, as if the sea belonged to the Turks, and as if the ships of no other nation had the right to sail upon it.

Charles V determined to capture Algiers and put a stop to the sufferings of the many thousand Christians whom the Turks kept in prison or slavery. With an army of over twenty thousand men he landed near Algiers, and it looked as though he would certainly take the city.

But the night before he intended to make the attack a storm arose. A torrent of rain fell. The soldiers had no tents, and they were drenched. The wind blew bitterly cold; and toward morning the Turks sallied forth from the gate of the city and, making a sudden attack upon the Christians, threw them into confusion.

Charles V himself mounted his horse and rallied the troops. But though they fought bravely they could not capture the city, and after losing several hundred men they retreated to their ships and sailed back to Spain.

Another of Solyman's pirate captains was Dragoot. He attacked two villages not far from Naples, and took about a thousand prisoners—men, women and children. Then he let the Christian people know that if they brought a sufficient sum of money they might ransom relatives or friends whom he had captured. He also told the Turks that they could buy his captives as slaves.

Thus both by sea and by land the Turks under Solyman were dreaded by the most powerful nations of Europe. But they were able to go no farther than Hungary, except on the one occasion when they attacked Vienna.

Being checked in Europe, Solyman turned his thoughts toward Asia, and with a powerful army he invaded Persia.

The Persians met him in battle; but finally the Persian monarch had to purchase peace by payment of a large sum of money. Except for this Solyman would certainly have taken possession of the whole country.

Solyman's promise to his father was well kept. He pushed the empire of Turkey westward into the heart of Europe, and eastward into the heart of Asia. He filled both continents with dismay.

But the end was near. In 1566 a revolution broke out in Hungary, and Solyman, at the head of a vast army, went to quell it. He was then a white-haired man of seventy-six, but vigorous and active. He rode at the head of his troops on a favorite black horse which had carried him in many a campaign. He was cheerful and hopeful, and as he went along he conversed with his officers.

"I must conquer the Hungarians this time so thoroughly," said he, "that they will never revolt again. Then I will return home and hang up my sword, for I am getting too old to bear the hardships of war."

He crossed the river Drave and laid siege to the fortress of Szigeth (se' get), which was defended by a small force of Hungarians. They gallantly resisted the attack of the Turks; but at the end of four weeks, were forced to surrender.

The conqueror, however, did not live to enjoy his victory. He was stricken with apoplexy and died while the siege was going on.

If Solyman had devoted himself to the advancement of his own people, instead of spending his life in fighting others, he might have done a great deal of good; for in the first years of his reign he made excellent laws. He tried to do justice to all; and he severely punished any officer of his kingdom who oppressed the people.

He was probably the greatest of all the sultans of Turkey.

CHAPTER 9

Sir Frances Drake

(1540-1596)

QUEEN ELIZABETH—POPULARLY known as "Good Queen Bess"—ascended the throne of England in 1558. Her reign was both magnificent and successful; and it added much to the greatness of the nation.

It was during Elizabeth's reign that England first became a great naval power; and among the men who helped to make her so, none were more famous than Sir Francis Drake.

There is some doubt about the date of Drake's birth. It is now generally believed that he was born in 1540, though some writers put the date at least five years earlier.

The place of his birth was the little town of Tavistock, in Devonshire. He seems to have had a great love for the sea even when but a child. His parents were too poor to help him into a good position, and so he began his career at sea as a cabin boy. But he had the merit of pluck; and he soon rose to the highest rank in the English navy.

In 1567 he went with his uncle Hawkins, who was one of the noted sailors of that day, on a slave-trading voyage to Africa and the West Indies. The experiences he met with at that time gave color to the rest of his life.

Being driven out of their course by storms, they were obliged to seek shelter in the harbor of San Juan de Ulua, a Spanish port on the coast of Mexico. There they were received with a show of kindness, but were afterwards attacked by a superior force, and only two vessels escaped.

After this act of treachery, Drake resolved to seize every opportunity to plunder the Spaniards and thus to make good the loss which he and his uncle had sustained.

In the years 1570–71 Drake made two other voyages to the West Indies for the purpose of becoming acquainted with the situation and strength of the Spanish settlements.

In 1572, he sailed again with two ships, one of seventy-five tons, the other of twenty-five. His plan was to capture the town of Nombre de Dios (nom' bra da dyos') on the Isthmus of Panama, which was the port from which the Spaniards shipped to Spain the gold and silver taken from the mines of Peru.

In the attempt to take this town Drake was severely wounded. He tried to conceal his hurt from his men; and they pressed onward into the town. But just as they reached the market place where they hoped to find the treasure, he fainted from loss of blood. His men at once carried him to his ship, and the enterprise was abandoned.

As soon as he was able to do so, he began to sail back and forth along the coast. He seized a large number of ships, and took from them a great amount of wealth both in money and goods.

He formed an alliance with a band of run-away slaves called Cimarrones (the ma ro' nes), and together they built a fort on a small island at the mouth of a river. There Drake and his men remained until February 3, 1573.

On that day Drake set out, with some Cimarrones as guides, to cross the Isthmus of Panama and gain his first view of the Pacific Ocean. Half way across the isthmus they led him to a tall tree standing on a central hill. Among the topmost branches of this tree there was a platform on which ten or twelve men might stand at ease. Drake climbed up to this platform, and was delighted to find that from his lofty perch he could see both the Atlantic and the Pacific.

Drake returned to England in the fall of 1573, carrying much treasure which he divided with the strictest fairness among his followers. His own share was large enough to enable him to purchase three ships. With these he sailed to Ireland, and there, as a volunteer under the Earl of Essex, he "did most excellent service."

But Francis Drake is chiefly distinguished as the first Englishman who sailed round the world. In December, 1577, with five little vessels, about the size of those of Columbus, he sailed out of the harbor of Plymouth.

It took him seven months to reach Patagonia, and there he remained for about nine weeks. Two of his ships had become so leaky as to be unfit for further service, and he was compelled to abandon them. The crews and stores were taken on board the other vessels and the fleet started out to sail through Magellan Strait in order to reach the Pacific.

It was sixty years since Magellan had passed through the strait, but Drake's was the first English expedition to follow the great Portuguese navigator over this route.

While the vessels were in the strait, one of those terrific storms arose for which the region of Cape Horn is still noted. One ship called the Marigold was never heard of again, and the crew of the Elizabeth were so disheartened by the terrible weather that they put about and returned to England.

Although Drake was left with but a single ship he would not give up the voyage. He made his way into the Pacific, and sailed northward along the coasts of Chile and Peru.

The Spaniards had already established colonies on the western shores of South America. Santiago had been founded nearly forty years before, and Lima was already a town of considerable size.

As Spain and England were not friendly toward each other, it was thought perfectly right to capture Spanish vessels and to plunder Spanish towns; and Queen Elizabeth had given Drake a commission, signed with her own hand, authorizing him to do this.

After plundering a number of the Spanish settlements he pursued his voyage until he reached the western coast of North America. Finding that his ship was again in need of repairs, he landed for that purpose at a point which has since been named Drakes Bay, a little to the north of San Francisco Bay.

From California he sailed across the Pacific and visited the Spice Islands and Java. Leaving Java he crossed the Indian Ocean and passed around the Cape of Good Hope into the Atlantic. Then, steering northward, he made his way back to England, reaching home exactly two years and ten months after starting on the voyage.

On his arrival a banquet was prepared on board the ship in which he had thus sailed round the world. Queen Elizabeth was one of the guests. In honor of his achievement she knighted him on the deck of his ship, and it was in this way that he came to be called Sir Francis Drake.

The little vessel had been so battered by the storms through which it had passed that it was unfit for further service. But Elizabeth gave orders that it should be carefully preserved as a monument to its famous captain.

One hundred years later it was found that the timbers were badly decayed. It was then broken up. One piece of the wood, that was still sound, was made into a chair for King Charles II, who afterwards gave it to the University of Oxford, where it can still be seen.

Drake at Cadiz

A few years later, Sir Francis rendered another valuable service to his native land. Philip of Spain equipped an enormous fleet for the purpose of invading England. Drake learned that the larger part of this fleet was in the harbor of Cadiz, making final preparations for the voyage.

He was then at Lisbon with thirty English war ships under his command. He at once sailed for Cadiz, and, on arriving, he sent a fire-ship among the Spanish vessels, burned nearly a hundred of them, and escaped from the harbor unharmed.

This delayed the sailing of the Spanish fleet for nearly a year, and when at length it approached the shores of England, Drake did more, perhaps, than any other man to bring about its overthrow.

The Spaniards had collected about one hundred and thirty vessels of war, and more than fifty thousand men, and to this array they gave the proud title of the "Invincible Armada." Thirty-five thousand men were to land at the mouth of the River Thames and another large force was to land farther to the north. Then a third force threatened the west coast. In this way England was to be attacked at three different points at the same time. The Spaniards thought that the English would be bewildered, and would surrender.

But all this great armament was not prepared without some news of it getting to England, and preparations were made to repel the foe.

Drake's Ships Returning from Cadiz

Troops were collected at Tilbury ready to attack the Spaniards in case they succeeded in landing. The queen on horseback reviewed them, and made a stirring speech. The merchants of London and other ports offered their ships to be used as ships of war; the rich brought their treasures; the poor volunteered in the army and navy. Thus the coast was well guarded and the number of vessels in the fleet was increased from thirty to one hundred and eighty.

These carried about sixteen thousand men—not half the number on board the enemy's fleet—but they were sturdy English fighters. Howard was Lord

High Admiral, and with him were Drake, Frobisher, and Hawkins, the most famous English mariners of the time.

One evening, late in July, 1588, beacon lights blazed all along the coast of the English Channel telling the news that the Spanish fleet was coming. Next morning, arranged in a crescent, the Armada moved up the Channel. Its line was seven miles long.

Spanish Ships under Fire

The English fleet sailed out from Plymouth. Its vessels were light, while those of the Spaniards were heavy, but more than this, the English ships were finely managed, and their guns were skillfully aimed, while most of the shots of the Spaniards went over the heads of the English.

The Spaniards tried to come to close quarters, but the English vessels were so steered that this could not be done. Day after day for a week the fighting continued.

The Spanish commander then led his fleet into the harbor of Calais on the French side of the Channel. He wished to get provisions and powder and shot. He also wished to get some small vessels—swift sailors—with which he might match the light ships of his adversaries.

The English fleet followed, but it would not be allowed by the French to attack the Spaniards in the harbor. To force them out into the open sea, the

English turned eight of their oldest and poorest vessels into fire ships. Tar, rosin and pitch were placed upon them. The masts and rigging were covered with pitch. Their guns were loaded; and thus, all ablaze, they were sent at midnight drifting into the harbor with wind and tide. This fire fleet did its work. It did not indeed fire any Spanish ship but it so alarmed the Spaniards that they sailed from the harbor into the open sea, and there the English attacked them. Many of their ships were disabled, and four thousand of their men were killed in one day's fighting.

At Close Quarters

Next day the Spanish commanders held a council of war. The question to be decided was whether to try to sail home through Howard's fleet or go round Scotland and avoid his guns. It was determined to attempt the voyage round Scotland. So the whole remaining Spanish fleet of perhaps one hundred and twenty vessels steered toward the north.

On the coast of Scotland, there are dangerous rocks, and when the shattered Armada neared the Orkney Islands, violent storms arose, which wrecked many of the ships. Thus nature finished what man had begun—the ruin of the most powerful fleet that ever had sailed from the shores of Europe. Only fifty-four vessels and about ten thousand men succeeded in returning to Spain. About eighty ships had been destroyed, and thousands of men had perished.

Ten years after the destruction of the Armada, Sir Francis made one more voyage to the West Indies. He still cherished the plan of seizing the town of Porto Bello on the Isthmus of Panama, and thus securing the gold and silver brought there for shipment to Spain.

He was, however, again doomed to disappointment. He was stricken with fever, and died on board of his ship, January 28, 1596.

His body was buried at sea. Lord Macaulay wrote these lines in reference to his burial:

> *The waves became his winding sheet:*
> *The waters were his tomb.*
> *But for his fame—the mighty sea*
> *Has not sufficient room.*

He left no children, but his nephew was made a baronet in the reign of James II. England will always remember with gratitude the services he rendered in the days of her struggle to become "mistress of the sea."

CHAPTER 10

Sir Walter Raleigh

(1552-1618)

ANOTHER famous Englishman who lived in the days of Queen Elizabeth was Sir Walter Raleigh. He was a soldier and statesman, a poet and historian, but the most interesting fact about him is that he was the first Englishman who attempted to plant colonies in the region now known as the United States.

He was born in Devonshire, England, in 1552. At about the time that he was growing up, great sympathy was felt in England for the Huguenots, as the French Protestants were called, and Raleigh enlisted as a volunteer in the Huguenot army. He was in France at the time of the massacre of St. Bartholomew, in 1572, but we do not know how long he remained there.

In 1580 he went to Ireland as captain of a company of a hundred men, to aid in putting down a rebellion there.

Returning to England at the age of thirty, he became one of Queen Elizabeth's courtiers. He constantly sought to please her. A story is told that one day when Elizabeth was out walking at Greenwich, she came to a muddy place. Raleigh was in attendance upon her, and quickly took off his costly coat and spread it over the mud so that it formed a carpet for the queen to walk on. This gallant act is said to have gained him high favor from Elizabeth.

Whether the story is true or not it is certain that for some years he was the greatest favorite at the court.

In Queen Elizabeth's reign the English began to take great interest in the new country of North America. Raleigh and his half-brother, Sir Humphrey Gilbert, obtained from Queen Elizabeth permission to colonize any land in North America which was not already claimed by a Christian nation.

Five ships were fitted out and sailed from England, in 1583, under the command of Gilbert. Raleigh was unable to go, but he bore a large part of the expense of the expedition.

Hardly had the voyage begun when one of the ships, owing to sickness among the crew, was obliged to return to England. Gilbert, with the other ships, kept on his course across the Atlantic, and at last reached Newfoundland, where he went on shore and took possession of the island in the name of Queen Elizabeth.

Gilbert now sailed onward with the fleet.

Raleigh's Gallant Act

Near Cape Breton Island, the largest vessel stuck in the mud, and was broken to pieces by the force of the waves; all but fourteen, out of nearly a hundred men on board, lost their lives. Gilbert thought that now it would be impossible to carry out the colonization plan, so with his three remaining ships he started back to England.

A terrible storm came on, but the vessels kept together for a time. When last seen, Gilbert was sitting in the stern of his ship, reading a book. He shouted to those on board the other ships, "We are as near to heaven by sea as by land."

During the night his ship disappeared, and not one on board was saved, but the other vessels succeeded in reaching England.

Raleigh was not discouraged by this failure. In the following year he sent to America another expedition.

In due time his vessels reached the coast of what is now known as North Carolina. Everybody was charmed with the beauty of the country. But after exploring the coast for some distance, and taking possession of the region in the name of Elizabeth, the expedition for some reason returned to England without making a settlement.

The description which the explorers gave of the country which they had visited interested Queen Elizabeth. As she was called the "Virgin Queen," Raleigh suggested that she should give her name "Virginia" to the newly discovered territory. She did this, and the state of Virginia, which formed part of the territory thus discovered, obtained its name in that way.

Raleigh soon organized a third expedition which sailed in 1585 with about a hundred colonists. Seven vessels carried them. The fleet was commanded by Sir Richard Grenville while the colonists were in charge of a noted soldier named Ralph Lane.

After a long voyage they reached Roanoke Island, on the coast of North Carolina. Grenville returned to England with the fleet, while Lane was left on Roanoke Island to establish a settlement.

The colonists probably quarreled with the Indians. Their provisions failed, and they could get none from the red men. No ship from England came with supplies, and the colonists were thoroughly discouraged.

The next year a fleet under command of Sir Francis Drake called there by chance, and all the colonists returned home.

One of them, named Thomas Hariot, in an account of the colony, spoke of a herb "called by the natives yppomoc," and told how it was smoked by them in pipes. This herb was tobacco. Hariot and his companions had learned to like it, and they carried quantity home with them.

This was the first Virginia tobacco imported into England. Some of it was given to Raleigh who smoked it in silver pipes. Queen Elizabeth also learned the art, and she made smoking fashionable among people of high rank in England.

In 1587 Raleigh sent out to Virginia a fourth expedition. It consisted of three ships carrying one hundred and fifty colonists under Captain White.

After landing his passengers White returned to England for supplies. When he got back to America, three years later, he found that the colonists had disappeared, and it was never learned what became of them. Thus failed Raleigh's last attempt to colonize Virginia.

So confident was he that the new world would be colonized, that he wrote of Virginia, "I shall yet live to see it an English nation." And this he did, for he lived until 1618, and Jamestown had then been founded ten years.

Raleigh Erects Queen Elizabeth's Standard in America

Raleigh Smoking Alarms His Servant

In return for his services in quelling the Irish rebellion the queen gave him a large grant of land in Ireland. The most interesting fact about this Irish property is that Raleigh raised there the first potatoes grown in Europe.

You have read how Philip II of Spain attempted, in 1588, to invade England with his famous Armada, and how that great fleet was destroyed. There was in England a great hatred of the Spaniards and a great desire to injure them.

At that time Spain claimed most of the new world so far as it had been explored, and her ships were all the time coming home laden with the products of her possessions, and particularly with silver from her mines.

Raleigh fitted out privateers to capture such vessels, and a large Spanish ship was taken. She was the most valuable prize which, up to that time, had ever been brought into an English port. The queen herself had an interest in the expedition and was greatly pleased with her share of the plunder.

Raleigh had still a great desire to plant colonies, and he now turned his attention to South America. He placed a vessel in command of a certain Captain Whiddon, and sent him, in 1594, to explore the region now known as Guiana.

Fabulous stories had been told of the amount of gold in this province. It was said that the king, when he was going to make an offering to his gods, covered his body all over with gold dust, and from this the Spaniards called him "El Dorado," that is, "the gilded man."

In 1595 Raleigh himself set sail with five ships for the land of "the Gilded King." He entered the mouth of the Orinoco and sailed up the great river for a distance of about four hundred miles. But the river rose so high that navigation was imperilled; and Raleigh therefore returned to the coast and soon afterward sailed back to England.

War with Spain still continued; and, in 1597, an English expedition under Howard and Essex was fitted out to attack Cadiz, a seaport on the Spanish coast. Raleigh was in one of the ships and rendered important service. The English destroyed or captured the ships of a large Spanish fleet in the harbor, and the city itself was surrendered.

This exploit was one of the most brilliant ever achieved by the English navy. After it, the Spaniards never regained their power upon the sea.

All through the reign of Elizabeth, Raleigh was highly esteemed by the queen and by the people. Up to the date of her death he was a member of Parliament. But, in 1603, James I succeeded Elizabeth. He disliked Raleigh, and therefore stripped him of all his offices and accused him of entering into a plot against the king.

Raleigh was arrested and brought to trial. One who was present wrote that when the trial began, he would have gone a hundred miles to see him hanged; but that before it closed, he would have gone two hundred to save his life.

Although nothing was proved against him, Raleigh was condemned to death. Only when he stood on the scaffold was his sentence changed to imprisonment for life.

For thirteen years he was confined in the Tower of London; and there he wrote his great work "The History of the World." It is reported that the Prince of Wales often visited him in the Tower, and said, "No man but my father would keep such a bird in such a cage."

In 1616 Raleigh was released so that he might go on another expedition to the golden land of Guiana and capture Spanish merchant vessels.

Raleigh Departing from His Wife

But disease broke out among his crews, and Raleigh himself was stricken down with fever before they reached the Orinoco. His son was killed in a fight with the Spaniards; and, in 1618, the poor father returned to England broken-hearted.

Shortly after his arrival he was arrested and condemned to die the very next morning under the sentence of death which had been passed upon him fifteen years before.

Even then his courage did not leave him. On the scaffold he asked to see the axe. "This gives me no fear," he said. "It is a sharp medicine to cure me of all diseases." To someone who told him to lay his head toward the north, he replied, "What matter how the head lies, so the heart be right."

Raleigh's attempts at colonization were the beginnings of the great movement which led to the establishment of the Thirteen Colonies; and those colonies formed the basis for the United States of America.

CHAPTER 11

Henry of Navarre

(1553–1610)

IN the year 1569 the Catholics of France and the Huguenots, or French Protestants, were engaged in a bitter and bloody war. Although religion played a great part in the war it was really more of a political than a religious struggle.

In the early summer of that year the Catholics won a great victory near the town of Jarnac (zhar' nack). Among those who fell in the battle was the great Protestant leader, Louis, Prince of Condé.

The remnant of the Protestant army lay in camp near the castle of Cognac (Con' yak). They were sad and dispirited. Suddenly trumpets and drums were heard in the distance; and a sentry announced that a band of soldiers was approaching. It was soon learned that they were Huguenots, and the defeated Protestants were very glad to see them.

They proved to be the escort of Jeanne d'Albert, Queen of Bearn, a little kingdom in the extreme southwest of France. The people over whom she ruled were Protestants; and as soon as she heard of the death of Condé she hastened to the Protestant camp.

The army was drawn up to receive her. Stepping forward, and holding her son by the hand, she said, "My friends, our cause has not died with the Prince of Condé. We have still left us brave captains. I offer to you as leader, Condé's nephew, my son, the Prince of Navarre."

With loud shouts of "Long live Henry, the Prince of Navarre," the soldiers at once elected him as their commander-in-chief.

Prince Henry was the son of Anthony of Bourbon and Queen Jeanne. He was born in 1553, and therefore was but sixteen years old when called to fill this high position.

He was too young to lead the troops in battle; but he was ready to learn how to do so. The brave Admiral Coligni (ko leen ye) agreed to instruct him, and to command the Protestant forces until he was able to do so.

Henry was a sturdy and well-grown lad. His life had been a simple one. His principal food had been the brown bread, the chestnuts, and such other plain fare as was eaten by the peasant boys who lived among the mountains of his mother's kingdom. He would have been glad to go out to battle at once; but the wise Coligni would not permit him.

Henry was very fond of reading. His favorite books were those containing the stories of the great conquerors of former times. He also read, many times over, the story of the good knight Bayard—the knight without fear and without reproach—who had lived not very long before.

When not yet twenty years old, Henry was married to Margaret of Valois (val' wa), sister of the king of France. It was hoped that this marriage would bring peace to the country. It failed to do so, and the war went on for thirty years.

Only a few days after the wedding bells had rung so joyously at Henry's marriage, a very sad event took place which filled Europe with horror.

At about four o'clock, one August morning, in the year 1572, the great bell on the Palace of Justice awakened the people of Paris; and the soldiers of the Catholic party began to attack the Huguenots. When news of this massacre reached other French cities similar attacks were made and a great many Protestants were slain. The number has been variously estimated, some authorities stating that about a thousand in all were killed, others that the number reached a hundred thousand.

This was called the massacre of St. Bartholomew, because it happened on St. Bartholomew's Day.

The young Prince Henry was kept a prisoner in the king's palace for nearly four years. Then he escaped and again became the leader of the Huguenots.

He was so anxious for the restoration of peace that he sent to the Duke of Guise, who commanded the Catholic army, this challenge: "I offer to end the quarrel. Either I will fight with you alone, or two on our side will fight with two on yours, or ten with ten, or whatever number you please; so as to stop the shedding of blood and the misery of the poor." But the duke would not accept the challenge, and the war went on.

Henry III, King of France, was a very weak and foolish man. So the Duke of Guise determined to dethrone him and make himself king.

As soon as King Henry learned of this, he sent an assassin to murder the duke. When he heard that Guise was dead, the king said to his mother, who was very ill: "How do you feel?" "Better," she answered. "So do I," said the king. "This morning I have become king of France again. The king of Paris is dead."

The friends of the murdered duke at once took up arms against King Henry; and the Sorbonne—the great religious authority in Paris—declared that the people were no longer bound to obey him.

Then Henry III turned for help to his cousin, Henry of Navarre. They agreed to fight side by side against those who had revolted; and many of the Catholics joined with the Huguenots in order to bring about peace.

The rebels attacked King Henry near the city of Tours; but the Prince of Navarre marched to his aid, and the rebel leader left the field in great haste.

As the rebels had failed to conquer the French king in battle, they determined to have him murdered. They found a man to carry out their plot. One morning, he gained admission to the king's presence by saying that he desired to see him on important business. As soon as they were left alone, the murderer handed Henry a letter; and while the king was reading it, he drew a knife from his sleeve and plunged it into his body.

A messenger was sent in haste to tell Henry of Navarre. As he entered the king's room the tears gushed from his eyes, and he kissed the dying man with great tenderness.

Many of the nobility of France had, by this time, come in to see their dying ruler; King Henry begged them to acknowledge Henry of Navarre as his lawful successor; and all present agreed to do so. So the Prince of Navarre became king of France, with the title of Henry IV.

The rebels were not satisfied with this arrangement, since the law of the kingdom declared that no man could be king unless he were a Catholic. They demanded that Cardinal de Bourbon, Henry's uncle, should be made king with the title of Charles I.

Preparations were made for a great battle near the town of Arques (ark). During the night the forces of the new king had dug trenches and thrown up earthworks so as to give them a greater advantage over the enemy.

Next morning a rebel sentry, who had been captured during the night, was brought before him. As they talked together the man said, "We are about to attack you with thirty thousand foot and ten thousand horse. Where are your forces?"

"Oh," said the king, "you do not see them all. You do not count the good God and the good right; but they are ever with me."

A bloody battle followed, in which the king gained a wonderful victory. Soon after this he was joined by a body of English and Scotch soldiers sent him by Queen Elizabeth of England; and his army was thus increased to over ten thousand men.

One day a carrier pigeon flew into the camp. It brought a strip of paper inclosed in a quill. On the paper were written the words, "Come, Come, Come."

The king at once understood that he was needed at Paris; for that city was now in the hands of the rebels. He therefore hastened to its relief.

The king was not yet prepared to capture Paris. But he attacked many other cities; and about twenty of them opened their gates and received him as their sovereign.

Then followed the famous battle of Ivry, in which the cannon, the colors, and nearly all the supplies of the rebels fell into the king's hands. On the rebel side the loss in killed, wounded and captured was over eleven thousand, while the king lost but five hundred men.

Very soon after the battle of Ivry, Cardinal de Bourbon died; and at about the same time the king laid siege to Paris which was still in the hands of the enemy.

Before closing up all the avenues of approach to Paris he wrote a letter to the governor of the city, in which he said: "I am anxious for peace. I love my city of Paris. She is my eldest daughter, and I wish to do her more favors than she asks." But it was all in vain, and the siege went on.

King Henry's army prevented the carrying of food into the city, and the people soon began to suffer. Bread gave out and the people were glad to eat rats, cats, dogs, horses, or anything else they could find to prevent starvation.

King Henry allowed the women and children to leave the city. He even permitted supplies to pass through his lines to relieve the besieged, saying, as he did so, "I do not wish to be king of the dead."

But just as Paris was on the point of surrendering, the Duke of Parma, one of the ablest generals in the service of Philip II of Spain, arrived before Paris with a large Spanish army and compelled Henry to raise the siege.

Henry IV at Ivry

The king now felt that the only way in which he could give peace to his people was by uniting himself with the Catholic Church; and this he determined to do.

At eight o'clock on the morning of July 23, 1593, robed in white satin, he marched with a bodyguard of soldiers to the church of St. Denis, near Paris. At the door of the church he was met by a cardinal, an archbishop, nine bishops and large numbers of clergy and monks.

"Who are you?" asked the archbishop.

"The king," replied Henry.

"What do you wish?" was the archbishop's next inquiry.

To this the king replied, "To be received into the Catholic Church." Then the king knelt and declared, his belief, after which the archbishop forgave and then formally received him.

After this ceremony Henry was anointed at Chartres (shart'r), and thus declared sovereign of the whole kingdom.

Henry's great desire now was to make his people prosperous. He once said "I wish every peasant in France to have a fowl in the pot every Sunday."

To avoid, as far as possible, all further wars about religion, he signed and published the famous Edict of Nantes, in 1595.

This royal decree gave the Protestants equal rights with the Catholics. The government agreed to pay the salaries of their clergy as well as those of the Catholics. The Protestant children were allowed to enter the universities and colleges; their sick were received into the hospitals; and the two great religious parties of the nation were placed upon a common footing.

The last years of King Henry IV were years of peace and prosperity. The farmers and trades-people were happy. The heavy debt which had lain for so many years upon France was entirely removed; and the taxes were reduced to a rate lower than ever before.

In the midst of this growing sense of security and comfort all France was suddenly shocked and distressed beyond measure. A madman, by the name of Ravaillac (ra-vi-rack'), stabbed the king to the heart; and the career of the noble and generous Henry of Navarre was at an end.

The Murder of Henry IV

CHAPTER 12

Wallenstein

(1583-1642)

A BLOODY religious war broke out in Germany in 1618, and as it lasted until 1648 it is called "The Thirty Years' War." This war was one of the most dreadful that ever raged in Europe. It was a struggle between the Catholic and Protestant parties, like that in France which we have read about in the story of Henry of Navarre.

Many Catholics and Protestants opposed each other because they wished to defend their belief as well as to convert others to it. But many of the princes and nobles used the disturbed religious conditions to increase their power. Thus religion and politics were closely united, and the lines were drawn between two great parties, the Catholic League and the Evangelical Union. Therefore all through those thirty years the Catholics and the Protestants of Germany strove with all their might to overcome and destroy one another.

Of course this great war required great leaders. The ablest general on the Catholic side was Albrecht von Wallenstein (fon wol' en stin), who was born in Bohemia in 1583. His parents were Protestants. They died while he was yet a child; and he was brought up by an uncle who was a Catholic.

This uncle sent him for his early education to the Jesuit College at Olmutz (ol' mutz), and afterwards to the universities of Bologna and Padua. While at the Jesuit College, Wallenstein became a Catholic, and this changed his whole career.

Wallenstein inherited from his father a large estate and an immense sum of money. By his marriage with an aged widow his wealth was nearly doubled; and when his uncle died and left him his property, Wallenstein became one of the richest men of his day.

His aged wife did not live long after their marriage, and he took for his second wife a daughter of the Count of Harrach. By this second marriage his wealth was again increased; and through his wife's father, he gained much influence and many friends at the court of Vienna.

After completing his education he traveled through Italy, Spain, France, and Holland. He served for a short time in Hungary in the army of the Emperor Rudolf who was then at war with the Turks. But as yet he did not display any marked ability as a soldier.

With a part of his wealth he purchased from the emperor of Austria, a vast territory in Bohemia and Moravia, at a cost of over seven million florins. To this territory he gave the name of Friedland, that is, Land of Peace.

The emperor gave him the title of Duke of Friedland; and he managed his duchy wisely and well. Justice was so faithfully administered in the courts that all men had their rights; and the farmers, miners, and manufacturers were properly cared for.

Beginning of the Thirty Years' War

When the "Thirty Years' War" broke out Wallenstein raised a regiment of dragoons to aid the cause of the emperor. He was also the means of saving the money in the imperial treasury from falling into the hands of the enemy.

As Wallenstein came more fully into notice his ambition steadily increased. In all that he did, he seemed to have an eye to his own advantage.

After the war had been going on for some time, the emperor found himself sorely in need of a better army. Then Wallenstein called upon him and said, "My liege, you shall have such an army as you require. I myself will bear the expense of equipping it. I make, however, this condition, that I shall have the right to compel the people in any part of the empire where my troops may be fighting to supply them with provisions;" and to this condition the emperor agreed.

Wallenstein soon made for himself a reputation as a great commander. There were plenty of men in Germany who were ready to fight for pay and plunder, and he therefore soon raised a force of over thirty thousand soldiers. He himself went with them to the front.

During the first two years Wallenstein and his men were everywhere successful, but at length they met with a severe check. They had laid siege to a large commercial city called Stralsund (stral' soond). This was one of the wealthiest ports on the Baltic. It exported a great deal of grain and other produce, and vessels flying its flag were seen in every harbor of Europe.

Wallenstein determined to capture Stralsund. His soldiers knew that if he succeeded, they would get a vast amount of plunder, and an abundance of provisions for their future use.

Wallenstein had more in mind than that. He planned to turn the merchant vessels of Stralsund into battle ships, and thus secure a fleet which would enable him to carry on the war by sea as well as by land. He would then attack the other great ports of Germany, such as Lubeck, Hamburg and Bremen.

All these ports had large fleets of merchant ships. He planned that after taking these he would make his navy the largest in the world. He even dreamed of capturing the ships of England, Sweden, and the Netherlands, and thus making himself master of the sea.

It was with these thoughts in his mind that Wallenstein laid siege to the great port of Stralsund. He swore that he would capture it "even if he found it to be fastened to heaven with chains of gold."

But Stralsund was well supplied with provisions; and, for eleven weeks, the brave citizens repelled his attacks. Wallenstein's men began to suffer for lack of food; and at last the great commander was forced to abandon the siege.

Living Off the Country

Every year a festival of rejoicing is still held in Stralsund to commemorate the day on which Wallenstein and his starving army retreated, baffled and angry, from before its walls.

Wallenstein had won so many victories that some of those who fought on his side had become jealous of him. As soon, therefore, as he met with this great reverse at Stralsund, his enemies persuaded the emperor to take the command of the army away from him.

They made the emperor believe that he was a very dangerous man, and that with his large army which had grown very fond of him, he meant to rule all Germany, and lord it over every prince and duke in the empire.

The emperor at once wrote him a letter ordering him to give up his command. Although greatly surprised, Wallenstein took his dismissal in silence. He bade farewell to his troops, and went to live quietly in the capital of his duchy.

Not long after Wallenstein had left the army the emperor found that he had made a mistake. Instead of hearing of victory after victory, he now received news of one defeat after another. His second-best general was fatally wounded; and he had no one like Wallenstein to put in command of the army.

After suffering a number of disastrous defeats the emperor sent to Wallenstein and begged him to take command once more. He gave him permission to choose his own officers, and to carry on the war just as he thought best. He also promised that, in future, no one should interfere with him.

On these terms Wallenstein again accepted the emperor's offer, and was soon back in the field at the head of an army of forty thousand men.

By this time, however, a greater general than even Wallenstein had become the leader of the Protestant forces. This was the famous Gustavus Adolphus, king of Sweden, whose bravery had already been shown on many a bloody field.

The two commanders and their armies met near a place called Lutzen (loot'sen), in Saxony, and there a fearful battle was fought.

In this battle Gustavus lost his life, but his army fought on nobly and won the day. The victory at Lutzen is always spoken of as the greatest victory of the "Thirty Years' War."

When Wallenstein found that the Protestant army had won the battle in spite of the loss of its commander, he became greatly troubled, and scarcely knew what to do. He seemed afraid to meet such an army again.

He doubtless saw that it was useless to continue the war, and hoped that the emperor would make terms to the Protestants, and so establish peace.

Wallenstein's enemies again appeared before the emperor with the old story that he was simply fighting for himself, and was determined to make himself ruler over the entire nation.

Strange as it may seem, the emperor again believed them. He even went so far as to call Wallenstein a traitor, and he caused him to be publicly disgraced and again removed from command.

With a guard of about a thousand men, and accompanied by several of his leading officers, Wallenstein left the camp and once more started for his home. He supposed that all who accompanied him were his faithful friends. But it was not so. Four of the men whom he thus trusted had already agreed to assassinate him. Having first murdered his real friends, they hurried to the house where Wallenstein was staying, broke into his room, and killed him as he was retiring to rest. It is said that, for this shocking crime, the murderers were handsomely rewarded by the emperor.

Wallenstein ranks as one of the world's greatest soldiers, rather than as one of its greatest heroes. His work was a hindrance rather than a help to human progress, and this it is which so largely dims his fame.

Assassination of Wallenstein

CHAPTER 13

Gustavus Adolphus

(1594-1632)

IN the year 1594 a child was born in the royal palace of Stockholm who was destined to have great influence upon the history of modern Europe.

He was the son of Charles IX, king of Sweden, and a grandson of the famous hero, Gustavus Vasa. He was given the name of Gustavus Adolphus.

As soon as he was old enough to begin his education he was provided with the best of teachers. He soon learned to speak Latin, Greek, German, Dutch, French, and Italian, but before he was eighteen his studies were brought to an end by the death of his father. He was at once proclaimed king of Sweden.

Gustavus had been carefully instructed in athletics, especially in riding, fencing, and military drill. He was a boy of muscle as well as of mind, and he soon proved the value of both.

At the time of his father's death, Sweden was at war with Denmark. The Danes had captured the two most important fortresses of Sweden. Gustavus was determined to win them back, and he continued the war with great vigor.

A few months after his accession the Danes sent a fleet of thirty-six ships against Stockholm, but Gustavus, marching night and day, led his army to a point from which he could attack the Danish fleet with advantage. A storm also hindered the Danes from landing, and they returned home disappointed.

When the king of Denmark heard of these rapid marches and found that he had no mere boy to contend with, he consented to a treaty of peace by which Sweden regained one of her fortresses and was permitted to buy back the other.

From 1614 to 1617, Gustavus was at war with Russia to recover the pay due to Swedish soldiers which his father had sent to Russia a few years before.

Gustavus Adolphus

In that war he took from Russia the two provinces of Carelia and Ingria. These provinces remained in the possession of Sweden for more than a hundred years, serving as a great barrier between Russia and the Baltic Sea. Even the land on which St. Petersburg now stands passed into the hands of the Swedes; and at the close of the war, Gustavus declared, "The enemy cannot now launch a boat on the Baltic without our permission."

When Gustavus came to the throne, Sweden was at war also with Poland. The cause of the war was this: Charles IX, the father of Gustavus, was not the true heir to the Swedish crown. It belonged, by right, to Sigismund, king of Poland.

Sigismund had tried to take the crown of Sweden from Charles; and he now tried to take it from Gustavus. But Gustavus won a great victory over Sigismund and forced him to abandon his claim to the throne and to make a peace which was of great advantage to Sweden.

Ten years before the birth of Gustavus a new star had suddenly appeared in the northern skies of Europe. The new star rapidly became one of the brightest in the firmament. It could be seen by men with keen eyes even in the day time. But it soon began to lose its brilliancy, and in about a year and a half it disappeared entirely. In those days, people thought that wonders in the heavens had much to do with events upon the earth.

When Gustavus Adolphus startled Europe by his brilliant victories over Denmark, Russia, and Poland, men began to believe that the wonderful star foreshadowed the wonderful boy king of Sweden. Some, however, began to speak of him as the snow king, and declared that he would soon melt. Finally, they came to think of him rather as one of the old Scandinavian war gods. In the end, they found that he was equal to greater tasks than those he had already accomplished.

The empire of Germany was, at that time, divided against itself. The "Thirty Years' War" was raging. The grain fields were trampled down by marching troops. Towns were besieged and burned. Innocent people were destroyed by thousands. Two great generals—Wallenstein and Tilly—were filling the empire with horrors.

In 1631 the city of Magdeburg was taken by Tilly. Its little garrison of twenty-four hundred men had made a noble defense, but Tilly had no respect for their bravery. As soon as the city fell into his hands he put these brave soldiers to death; and during the next two days his soldiers pillaged the city and slaughtered more than twenty thousand of the inhabitants.

All Europe was horrified. Gustavus Adolphus gathered an army of thirteen thousand chosen men and at once invaded Saxony. On the outskirts of the little town of Breitenfeld, not far from Leipzig, Gustavus met the inhuman Tilly and defeated him in battle.

The people of Saxony were wild with delight. They gladly opened the gates of their cities to welcome the conqueror of the dreaded Tilly. Thousands flocked to the standard of Gustavus and his army was soon more than four times as large as when he had left Sweden.

Tilly at Magdeburg

With this large body of fresh troops at his command, Gustavus determined to follow the German army which had retreated into Bavaria. Having overtaken the Germans, he at once put his army into line and began the attack. In the desperate battle which ensued Tilly was mortally wounded; and he died as he was being carried from the field.

It was at this time that the emperor recalled Wallenstein and again placed him in command of the German army, as we have read in the previous story.

It was not long before Gustavus and Wallenstein found themselves face to face upon the field of combat. They met in battle near Lutzen, in Saxony, to which place Gustavus had returned on account of the large number of Saxons in his army.

During the morning a thick fog hung over the field and the fighting did not begin until nearly noon. Then, as the skies cleared, the king and his army approached the German lines singing Luther's beautiful hymn, "A mighty fortress is our God." As they ceased singing, Gustavus waved his sword above his head and cried, "Forward! in God's name," and the battle began.

In one particular Gustavus was most imprudent. A wound, received some time before, made it painful for him to wear a breastplate; and so he led his troops into the engagement, wearing a common riding coat.

Early in the afternoon his arm was pierced by a ball from a pistol, and this probably severed an artery. For a time he concealed his wound and continued to encourage his men. But he grew faint from loss of blood, and finally said to one of the princes riding near him, "Cousin, lead me out of this tumult. I am hurt."

As they turned, a musket ball struck the king in the back, and he fell to the ground dying.

Some of Wallenstein's men rode up and inquired his name. "I am Sweden's king," he replied. "I am sealing the religion and the liberty of the German nation with my blood."

When the troops of Gustavus learned of his death, they attacked the enemy with such fury that Wallenstein was quickly defeated; and Gustavus won the battle despite the loss of his life.

In Gustavaus it it said the star in the north had become the most brilliant in the heavens; and just as suddenly its light was quenched. The snow king had melted at last.

A great work had been done, however. Gustavus and his brave band of Swedes had inspired half a continent with hope and courage. His splendid victories also did much to crush the tyrannical power of Germany; and the good which this great man accomplished had much to do with the spreading of religious liberty over Europe.

Body of Gustavus Adolphus On Its Way to Sweden

After the battle was over, and just as twilight was gathering, the body of the hero was carried into a little church nearby and laid before the altar. The soldiers, still dressed in their armor, were the chief mourners; and a village schoolmaster read the simple service for the dead.

Next morning the body was embalmed, and the soldiers carried it back to Stockholm. There it was laid to rest in the church of Riddarholm which contains the royal tombs, and where many others of the greatest and best men of Sweden are buried.

CHAPTER 14

Cardinal Richelieu

(1585-1642)

WHILE Wallenstein on the one side, and Gustavus Adolphus on the other, were fighting the battles of the "Thirty Years' War" in Germany, a similar religious war was going on in France. Louis XIII and his famous prime minister, Richelieu, were fighting with the Huguenots, or Protestants of France.

Louis sat on the throne, but the real ruler of France was Cardinal Richelieu. The full name of the Cardinal was Armand de Richelieu; Richelieu being the name of his father's estate, upon which, in 1585, Armand was born.

When he was twenty-two he entered the ministry and soon became a bishop. His people were mostly poor; and Richelieu felt that there was a grander career before him than to remain their bishop.

He determined to make something of himself, and to be the equal of any nobleman in the kingdom. There was only one way in which he could do this. That was by becoming a politician. His ambition was to become a leader of men.

In Richelieu's time, there was an assembly in France called the states-general. It was composed of delegates who represented the nobles, the clergy, and the commons—the three great classes into which the nation was divided.

But the states-general had no real power. It did not, like our congress, make laws. It could only petition the king. The delegates presented addresses to His Majesty, telling him of any trouble in the kingdom and begging him to remedy it.

Cardinal Richelieu

This gave him a good opportunity to win the favor of Louis XIII's mother, the famous Marie de Medici, who was acting as regent of the kingdom until Louis should come of age. The young orator could not say enough in her praise, and she naturally took a liking to him.

About a year after his oration at the meeting of the states-general, Richelieu was invited by the queen mother to become a member of the council of state. He remained in the council, however, only a short time; for a quarrel arose between the king and his mother, and Richelieu retired from office.

Soon, however, the death of Luynes (lu'een), a favorite minister of Louis, gave him the opportunity to return to Paris. He again took a position under the king, and became the most valuable officer that Louis ever had.

When Henry of Navarre granted to the Huguenots the celebrated Edict of Nantes, the French people generally hoped that the religious troubles in France were forever ended. But unfortunately, this was not the case. In 1621 some of the Huguenots held a great meeting at La Rochelle, which was their richest city, and there made a kind of declaration of independence.

Louis VIII and Richelieu

The king of France had several fortresses in that part of the country. One of these, called "St. Louis," commanded La Rochelle.

King Louis considered that he had a right to maintain fortresses anywhere in France, but the Huguenots insisted that the fortress of St. Louis should be demolished. The king, instead of pulling it down, made it stronger.

The Huguenots then did a very unwise thing. In 1622 they rose in a general revolt, and made an attack on some of the king's war vessels and captured them. Richelieu, however, managed to put down the revolt.

Two years later the English made war upon France and again the Huguenots revolted. Richelieu then decided that their power must be destroyed.

So with an army of twenty-five thousand men he marched to La Rochelle and besieged it. The city was well protected. On the land side were vast swamps through which an army could neither march nor drag siege guns. An attack might have been made by sea, but at that time the king had no navy.

Richelieu on the Dike at La Rochelle

To prevent food being taken into the city across the marshes was easy; but the only way to prevent its going in by ships was to close the harbor. To do this, a great stone dike, a mile long, was built across the channel that led to the city.

Richelieu paid his men twice ordinary wages, and in that way, although it was winter, he succeeded in getting the work done. The harbor was thus practically closed. Food soon became scarce, and great suffering prevailed in La Rochelle.

But no one thought of surrender. The women were just as determined to hold out as were the men. Months passed, and still the siege went on. The starving citizens hoped every day to see an English fleet come to their aid; and an English fleet did come.

When the English commander learned of the great dike that Richelieu had built, he was afraid to approach it lest his ships should be wrecked. He therefore sailed away without firing a gun.

At the close of the summer the besieged were obliged to eat horses, dogs, and cats. It is said, that they boiled the skins of these animals, and even boiled old leather trying to make it fit for food.

In September a second English fleet attempted to enter the harbor; but by this time Richelieu had equipped a number of large war vessels, and the English met with determined resistance. A storm damaged many of their vessels, and the battered fleet was forced to sail back to England. By this time one half of the population had died; and, of those left, few were strong enough to do military duty.

At length after a siege of fifteen months, La Rochelle surrendered, and the king made a triumphal entry into the city. The fortifications were destroyed, and the power of the Huguenot nobles was forever at an end.

Richelieu compelled the nobles to admit that Louis was master of France. Many of them, however, were extremely angry at the loss of their power, and conspiracies against the life of Richelieu were more than once formed; but he always managed to find out about them and to punish those engaged in them. Many of the conspirators were executed; and thus Richelieu's power was actually increased instead of destroyed.

It should be said that though Richelieu destroyed the fortresses of the Huguenots, he was not unfair to them about their religion. They were allowed to worship God according to their own consciences; for he was wise enough to know that people cannot be forced to worship in ways they do not like.

While Richelieu wished the king of France to be strong, he wished his neighbor, the emperor of Germany, to be weak. So in the same year in which he had broken down the power of the Protestant nobles, he actually gave help to the Protestant princes of Germany, who were fighting against the emperor just as the Huguenots had fought against King Louis.

He not only persuaded the great Gustavus Adolphus to lead his army of Swedes against the emperor, but he paid large sums of money to him for the support of his troops. Thus the great victories of Gustavus Adolphus, which were so valuable to the German Protestants, were won in part by soldiers paid and fed by Richelieu and the king of France.

Richelieu saw that if the emperor of Germany should overcome the Protestant princes and make himself head of the whole country, and as absolute as Richelieu had made Louis, Germany would be a more powerful country than France. Then Germany might take to herself some of the territory of France. Richelieu fought the Protestants in France to make France united and strong; he paid and fed the Protestant armies in Germany to keep Germany divided and weak.

While Richelieu was prime minister of France, the English and Dutch were planting colonies in America; and commerce in the fish and furs which were brought from the New World was becoming very active and profitable.

Richelieu desired France to be the equal of England as a colonizing and commercial nation. He therefore gave a charter to the Company of "New France," as Canada was often called. He granted to the Company the sole right to collect furs in America, and the sole right to sell them in France. In return, the Company was required within fifteen years to land at least four thousand colonists in Canada.

To protect trading vessels from pirates who then infested the seas, to defend the coast of France, and to protect her colonies, Richelieu saw that a navy was required. He created the navy of France. When Louis XIII came to the throne the country had not a single war ship. When he died, the French navy consisted of twenty men-of-war and eighty smaller vessels.

Long before Richelieu died he had accomplished the object of his life. He had made the king of France an absolute monarch, and himself as absolute as the king.

Wallenstein had desired to accomplish the same thing in Germany, but he had miserably failed. Charles I was trying to make his power absolute in England, but the English people rebelled against him.

Many years after the death of Richelieu, the Czar, Peter the Great, visited Paris. As he stood before the splendid marble monument of Richelieu, he exclaimed, "Thou great man! I would have given thee one half of my dominions to learn from thee how to govern the other half."

CHAPTER 15

Galileo

(1564-1642)

SOMETIME in the year 1583, repairs were going on in the cathedral of an old Italian city called Pisa; and, accidently, a workman had set swinging a great lamp which was suspended from the high roof of the building. People came into the church and knelt for a few minutes to say their prayers and then went out without noticing that the lamp kept on swinging to and fro.

A young man about eighteen years of age came into the church. He noticed the swinging lamp; and he also thought that it took just the same time to make each of its swings.

With his right hand he clasped his left wrist. He knew that the times between pulse beats are practically equal. So, feeling his pulse and watching the swinging lamp, he was trying to measure the one by the other.

The young man who watched the swinging lamp was Galileo; and he found that its motions were equal in duration.

Before his time no pendulum had ever swung in a clock. No clock with a pendulum had been thought of. But after Galileo published his great discovery that pendulums made their swings in equal periods of time, a man named Huygens (Hi' genz) made a pendulum clock.

It was found that pendulums about a yard long make each swing in a second; and so, at first, clocks were made with pendulums which beat seconds.

From Galileo's watching the swinging lamp, all our clocks may fairly be said to have been invented.

The father of Galileo hoped that his son would become a physician; but the young man liked to study mathematics, and his father permitted him to follow the bent of his genius.

Not long after graduating at the university, and when not quite twenty-five, Galileo was made professor of physics. He taught his classes about pumps and machinery, why smoke rises in the air, why birds' wings enable them to fly, and why fishes' fins send them through the water.

Nobody in Europe at that time knew much about such matters. There were no steam engines; no railroad trains were in existence; no steamers were crossing the seas.

People knew very little about such simple things as the falling of stones and feathers, and pieces of iron and lead. Even learned men thought that two pounds of lead would fall twice as fast as one pound, one hundred pounds one hundred times as fast, and so on.

One day Galileo asked some of his friends to climb with him the leaning tower of Pisa. This tower is one of the famous buildings of Europe. The odd thing about it is that it does not stand up straight like the tower or spire of a church, but leans over, as some of our trees do.

Some of Galileo's friends stayed at the foot of the tower; some went to the top. Heavy and light things were carried up and dropped from the summit of the tower; and one pound of iron reached the ground at the same instant as did a piece that weighed ten pounds.

While Galileo was professor at Pisa the people of Europe who watched the heavens saw a new star in the sky.

"Have you seen the new star? What do you think it is?" were questions that everybody was asking. Some thought it was only a meteor; but Galileo said, "No! It must be a star, because a meteor would surely be moving, and that star seems still." He gave three lectures upon it and people went by hundreds to hear him.

Galileo, like everybody else, could look at the star only with the naked eye. He tried to contrive something that would show both it and the other stars more plainly. He had seen spectacles. His grandfather wore a pair. He had somewhere read that if two eyeglasses are placed one above the other, things seen through them will appear nearer and larger.

Some bright man in Holland fixed an eyeglass at one end of a tube and another like it at the other end; and so made the first telescope.

Galileo And His Telescope

Galileo had heard about this. He bought a piece of lead pipe and fixed a glass at either end. His telescope magnified only three times; but it made things look nearer and larger.

He was as pleased with it as a child with a new toy. Wealthy and noble Venetians looked through it with wonder; just as when you look through a microscope at the point of a needle you are surprised to see how blunt it is.

Then Galileo used stronger lenses. His second telescope magnified eight times; and a third was made which magnified thirty times.

He looked at the moon; and he saw what no human being had ever seen before. There are mountains on the moon. He saw their bright tops and the shadows which they threw.

Then he looked at the planet Venus. She no longer looked like the other stars; but sometimes she seemed to be round like the full moon, sometimes horned, like the old and new moons.

With his naked eye Galileo counted only six stars in the Pleiades. People long years before had seen seven; and it was believed that one had been lost. Galileo looked one bright night and his telescope showed him forty. He looked at the Milky Way and found that its whiteness is the dim light of millions of stars so far away that they seem as small as the finest dust.

Galileo Showing the Heavenly Bodies Through the Telescope

He then made a fourth and larger telescope, and turned it upon the farthest away of the known planets. Jupiter, like Venus, seemed no more a star. It was round like the moon at the full.

But another and greater wonder appeared. Close to the edge of Jupiter's disk were three tiny stars. Two were seen on the east side of the planet and one on the west. They were Jupiter's moons.

Galileo watched on another night and found that instead of three there were four. We now know that there are seven.

He told the other professors in the university what he had seen, and the news quickly spread. The newly-found moons were called planets, just as our own moon was; and so it seemed that Galileo had made the number of planets eleven, instead of seven.

One of the professors was so angry that he would not even look through the telescope. Another man said, "The head has only seven openings—two eyes, two ears, two nostrils and one mouth, and how can there be more than seven planets?"

Galileo had an old friend called Kepler, who was the greatest astronomer then living. Galileo wrote to him, "Oh, my dear Kepler, how I wish we could have one good laugh together. Why are you not here? What shouts of laughter we should have at their glorious folly!"

About sixty years before this, Copernicus had printed a book in which he said that the earth was not still, as people thought, but that it was all the time moving round the sun.

Galileo did not at first believe this, and said in one of his letters that it was "folly." Then he saw that it was probably true; and when he looked through his telescope at the planets he became certain of it.

Milton Visiting Galileo At Florence

When people said that the system of Copernicus was contrary to the teaching of the Scriptures, Galileo tried to explain the sense in which the passages in the Bible are to be taken. He was then accused of teaching what would do harm to religion, and was summoned to Rome His trial took place in 1616 and he promised to give up his opinions concerning the Copernican system.

But his enemies still pursued him, and in 1633 Galileo was again accused of heresy and of breaking the promise he had made in 1616. The main part of the charge was that Galileo had denied that God is a personal being and that miracles are not miracles at all. As to breaking the promise he had made in 1616, Galileo admitted that he had felt proud of his arguments in favor of the Copernican system and in one of his books he had made out rather a strong case for it. He denied, however, having expressly taught the Copernican system. Unfortunately Galileo did not tell the truth in thus denying what he had taught, and he was sentenced to an indefinite term of imprisonment.

The imprisonment was not severe, although Galileo complained of it. He was to remain with an old friend and disciple; but at the end of six months he was permitted to return to his home near Florence.

His friends were allowed to visit him; but he was not allowed to go outside the gate to visit them. This was sad for him; but sadder still was the loss of his sight; for his eyes had seen more of the glory of the heavens than all the millions of eyes that had ever looked at the stars since the world began.

He died in 1642 and his body was interred in the Cathedral of Santa Croce.

CHAPTER 16

Louis XIV

(1638-1715)

AFTER the death of Richelieu, in 1642, Louis XIII, king of France, followed the advice of his great prime minister and called Cardinal Mazarin to fill his place.

But Louis XIII lived only six months after Richelieu passed away. He died in 1643, and his son Louis XIV succeeded him as king.

Louis XIV had the longest and most brilliant reign in the history of France; and the French people have always called him "The Grand Monarch."

He was born in 1638, and became king when he was but five years old. His mother governed the kingdom, as regent, until he was thirteen; but Mazarin was retained in office, and quickly became the real ruler of France.

Mazarin was a great statesman, but he was determined to have his own way. Many of the things he did cost a great deal of money; and so he made the people of France pay very heavy taxes, and this caused them to dislike him exceedingly.

Finally they became so discontented that they began a revolt known as the War of the Fronde, which means the War of the Sling. The name was given to ridicule the revolting party who were chiefly peasants; and who were too poor to buy proper arms. They were compared to the disorderly boys of Paris who sometimes fought with slings, and the name arose in that way.

This war lasted four years, and at its close Mazarin was dismissed. But he was soon put into office again, and had even more power than before.

As a boy Louis XIV was more fond of military exercises than of study. He took great delight in handling swords and beating drums. The boys belonging to some of the noble families of France were the playmates of the young king; and he formed them into a company of soldiers, and spent some time every day in drilling them.

In 1651, when he reached the age of thirteen, he took the government into his own hands, but Mazarin remained prime minister.

One of the first things Louis did, after declaring himself king, was to go with General Turenne into the South of France upon a military expedition. He was greatly pleased with life in the army and came back to Paris enthusiastic about military tactics.

Reception of Turenne By Louis Xiv at Versailles

"General Turenne," said the young king, "when I make war you must lead my troops."

"I deeply thank you, Sire, for your good opinion of me," replied the famous general. "I should be glad indeed to have command of Your Majesty's army in any war in which you may be engaged."

"Well, general," said Louis, "I feel sure that I shall have lots of wars; and you must be ready to help me."

Years afterwards Louis's words came true. He carried on many wars; and in some of them Turenne won fame as one of the greatest commanders of his time.

Louis saw that Mazarin was managing the affairs of the nation with great skill; so he allowed him to do as he thought best, while His Majesty devoted himself to a life of pleasure.

But in 1661, when Louis was twenty-three, Mazarin died. The day after Mazarin's death the officers of the government assembled at the palace, all eager to know which of them was to be the new prime minister.

"To whom shall we speak in the future about the business of the kingdom?" asked one of them.

"To me," answered the king. "Hereafter I shall be my own prime minister."

After thus taking matters into his own hands he reigned for more than fifty years. He placed in control of the different departments of the government the best men he could find; and one of his officers, the famous Colbert, managed the money matters of the kingdom in such a manner as to make his name illustrious for all time. He made the taxes less burdensome to the people; and, at the same time, he so fostered the industries of the kingdom that the revenue was greatly increased.

Louis improved the condition of the French people. He encouraged manufacturers. He even established some factories at the expense of the government; so that, during his reign, France became famous for her woolens and carpets, her silks and tapestries.

Louis also founded schools and colleges. He improved the country roads. He began the great canal which connects the Mediterranean with the Bay of Biscay. He did all in his power to advance the welfare of the kingdom.

At Versailles, a few miles from Paris, he built the largest and most magnificent palace in France. He adorned it with paintings and statues and surrounded it with lovely gardens. There he lived in great splendor, and gathered about him a large company of talented men and beautiful women.

The Louvre, the Trianon, the Tuileries, and some other of the most beautiful buildings for which Paris is still noted were also built during his reign.

In 1685, Louis revoked the famous Edict of Nantes, under which Henry of Navarre had granted religious liberty to the French people.

In consequence over three hundred thousand Protestants left France. They carried with them their tools and their trades and moved into other countries. More than forty thousand of them settled in England, where they were received with open arms. In his later life Louis had the same fondness for war as in his youth; and during nearly fifteen years he was engaged in wars with various European nations.

His army was large and thoroughly disciplined. He had also a navy which made France powerful on the ocean. He used to say with great pride, "I can fight the world equally well on the sea or on the land."

Wars were fought with Spain, Holland, England, Germany, and other nations, and brilliant victories were won.

These successes delighted the French people, and they almost adored their "Grand Monarch." Louis XIV became almost as much the terror of Europe as did Napoleon about a hundred years later; and then the decline began.

Among the men who helped to break down the military glory of Louis XIV, was Prince Eugene of Savoy.

Prince Eugene was born in Paris, in 1663. As soon as he was old enough for military service he asked King Louis to make him an officer in the French army.

Louis was not friendly to Eugene's mother, and the request of the young prince was refused. Indignant at this, Eugene left France; but he was determined to be a soldier somewhere.

He was twenty years old when the Turks laid siege to Vienna, and he was among the soldiers who helped to drive them back. His bravery brought him into notice, and he rapidly rose from rank to rank. At twenty-one he was a colonel, at twenty-two a major general, and at twenty-four a lieutenant general.

After serving in numerous battles against the Turks, Prince Eugene was sent, in command of an Austrian force, into Northern Italy, where Louis XIV was threatening the province of Savoy.

Eugene now had one of the great satisfactions of his life.

When Louis had refused him a commission in the French army he had said that he would never again enter France except as a conqueror. After several victories in Italy, he marched into France, captured several towns, and returned to Italy laden with great plunder, thus making good his word.

But the most important thing achieved by Eugene and his allies during this war with Louis was the capture of a strongly fortified town called Casal (ka' sal). This town stood near the borders of France and Italy, and commanded the easiest and most frequently traveled pass between the two countries.

When the town was taken, Eugene made it one of the conditions of surrender that its fortifications should be destroyed and never rebuilt.

Yet this did not prevent Louis XIV from making other attempts to capture Northern Italy; and Prince Eugene afterwards served in two other long wars that were successfully fought in its defense.

Louis continued fighting against Italy, Bavaria, and the Netherlands, and kept all Europe in a state of turmoil.

Then came the great battle of Blenheim (blen'im), in 1704.

Louis had made himself so obnoxious, and had become so dreaded, that a great league of the European nations was formed against him.

In the battle of Blenheim the English, under the Duke of Marlborough, united their forces with those of the Austrians under Prince Eugene.

The defeat of Louis XIV, on this occasion, was one of the most disastrous ever suffered by the French; and it greatly encouraged those who were defending the liberties of Europe. Louis's power in Bavaria and Holland was shattered, and his armies were never again so much of a terror as they had been.

Louis did not, however, give up at once. Fighting continued for about ten years longer; but there were no further victories for France.

When the war was ended, in 1713, by the peace of Utrecht (u' trekt), the French were obliged to give up to the British, Acadia, the Hudson's Bay Territory and Newfoundland. Austria also was given possession of some of the territory which had been held by France.

Battle Blenheim

A year later, in 1714, by the Treaty of Rastatt (ras tat), it was agreed that all the different nations which had been engaged in the war should have just what belonged to them before the war began.

The glory of France and her "Grand Monarch" had departed. He lived only a little more than two years after peace was proclaimed.

He died on September 1, 1715, at the age of seventy-seven, having reigned seventy-two years.

CHAPTER 17

Sir Isaac Newton

(1642-1727)

IN 1642, the very year in which the great Civil War broke out between Charles I, of England, and his Parliament, a wonderful man was born, named Isaac Newton.

As an infant he was so feeble that none of his family expected that he would live. If he had been a Spartan baby he would, according to Spartan law, certainly have been put to death. But by extra care on his mother's part his life was saved, and he grew into a lad with more than the ordinary powers of strength and endurance.

He was born in Woolsthorpe, in Lincolnshire, just one year after the death of Galileo, to whom he may be said to have borne a strong mental likeness.

When he first entered school he did not seem to be a very bright lad; but this was because he was not really trying to do his best.

One day a boy who ranked above him in his class struck him a severe blow. This proved to be one of the best things that ever happened to young Newton; for, feeling that he was no match for the other lad with his fists, he determined to get even with him by beating him in the work of the class. This he soon did; and then he rose higher and higher until he stood above all the other boys in the school.

He spent most of his play hours in making mechanical toys. He watched some workmen who were putting up a windmill near his school; and then made a working model of it and fixed it on the roof of the house in which he lived.

Isaac Newton

He constructed a clock which was worked by a stream of water falling upon a small water wheel. He also built a carriage and fitted it with levers so that he could sit in it and move himself from place to place. This was, perhaps, the first velocipede ever constructed.

In Newton's day gas lamps and electric lights were unknown. The winter days were short, and it often happened that he had to go to school in the dark. So he made for himself a paper lantern to give him light on his early journeys, and this was soon copied by the other boys.

In the yard of the house in which his parents lived he traced on a wall, by means of fixed pins, the movements of the sun. Clocks were then very expensive, and the contrivance, which received the name of "Isaac's dial," was a standard of time to the country people of the neighborhood.

When he was fourteen his stepfather died, and his mother thought it best for Isaac to work upon a farm which belonged to the family. So he left school; but he had no love for plowing and reaping, or for attending to horses, cows, and pigs.

The sheep went astray while he was thinking out some problem in algebra or geometry; and the cattle got into the standing crops and munched the milky wheat-ears while he was studying the motions of the moon, or wondering what made the earth go round the sun.

His mother soon saw that Isaac would never make a farmer. He was therefore sent back to school and fitted to enter college.

He was the most wonderful mathematician that ever graduated from the University of Cambridge; and, when only twenty-seven, he was made professor of mathematics in the college in which he had studied.

He rose to eminence in the university, and through the influence of some of its leaders he was appointed Warden of the Mint in 1695, and was promoted to the Mastership four years later.

He then moved to London, and went to live in a little house near Leicester Square. His salary enabled him to devote himself to his favorite studies; and this he proceeded to do.

One of the first important discoveries he made was about light.

Before his time every one thought that light was made up of fine lines, or rays; bright, but without any color.

Isaac made an experiment which any boy can repeat. He bored a small hole through the shutter of a window so as to allow only a delicate pencil of light to enter the room. This made a round spot of white or colorless light on the wall opposite the window; and he set out to examine this spot and see what it could teach him.

Newton and the Prism

When he put a glass prism into the pathway of the ray, he found that the colorless spot disappeared. Instead of it he saw on the wall, above where the circular spot had been, a beautiful band of light in which several colors were blended. At the top end this band was blue. At the bottom it was red. In the middle it was yellow.

Newton had thus discovered that a ray of white light is made up of colored rays.

His next experiment was with soap bubbles.

He found that when blown very thin the colors of the light could be more plainly discerned, and he was soon able to count seven distinct tints violet, indigo, blue, green, yellow, orange and red. These are the seven colors seen in the rainbow.

But the greatest of Newton's discoveries was that which is now spoken of as "The Law of Gravitation."

Everybody knew, long before Newton was born, that apples fell from trees to the ground: but no one seems to have asked the question why they never moved the other way.

All boys know that a ball thrown up into the air will come down again: but no one, before Newton lived, had tried to find out why this was so.

At first he seems to have thought that only things that were near to the earth would fall to its surface. But when he thought how the rain drops fell from the clouds he saw that his theory was not true.

Then he thought of the moon going round the earth; and wondered how it kept just so high up in the sky; and why it did not fall like the rain drops. This was a new puzzle and he set to work to solve it.

About two hundred years before Isaac Newton was born, a great Polish astronomer named Copernicus had written a book in which he had said that people were wrong who believed that the sun goes round the earth.

Copernicus insisted that the earth moves round the sun. At the first people made fun of this idea, but by Newton's day they had begun to believe it. Isaac began to wonder if this theory might not help him to solve his problem.

One of the favorite games of the boys of that day was to throw stones with a sling. Doubtless Isaac had himself used one many times in his play.

Now that he was grown up he remembered how he had whirled the stones round and round at a high rate of speed; and yet they never left the sling until he let go one of the strings.

Isaac knew that the moon goes whirling round the earth at the rate of about fifty thousand miles every day; and that the earth whirls round the sun at the rate of about one thousand miles a minute.

Certainly, thought Newton, the moon goes round the earth, and the earth goes round the sun, just as a stone is whirled round in a sling; but there must be something stronger than a cord to keep them in their places.

After thinking about the matter for a long time, he said, the moon is drawn toward the earth by a very powerful force; but she does not come nearer to the earth, or fall upon it, any more than the stone in the sling falls upon the hand of the slinger, because, like the stone, 'she is in rapid motion.

The earth is drawn toward the sun by the same wonderful force that draws the moon toward the earth; yet the earth does not fall upon the sun because it is all the while whirling forward at the rate of a thousand miles a minute.

Newton saw that the force which brings the stone and the apple down to the ground is the very same that draws the moon toward the earth and the earth toward the sun. He called this force "Gravity," or force of weight.

Then his great mind went on thinking beyond the moon and the earth to the far away stars. He soon learned that the same force which keeps the moon and the earth in their orbits, keeps all the stars of the sky in their courses.

For his great discoveries he was highly honored by the learned men of his day. He was made a member of the Royal Society, a society established for the purpose of gathering up and treasuring all forms of valuable knowledge.

The Royal Society aided him in publishing his books, of which he wrote twelve. The most important of these is called the "Principia."

In 1705 he was knighted by Queen Anne; and when he died, in 1727, his body lay in state for a whole week in the Jerusalem Chamber; and was then buried with great pomp in Westminster Abbey.

CHAPTER 18

William III

(1650-1702)

THE story of King William's life is an interesting one. He was born in Holland in 1650, and was a prince of the distinguished house of Orange, which for many years had been prominent in the history of the Netherlands.

William was carefully educated. He showed so much ability that when he was only twenty-two years old he was chosen stadtholder, or president of the Netherlands.

In 1672, Louis XIV, with an army of one hundred and twenty-five thousand men, under the command of Turenne and Condé, invaded the Netherlands. England united her forces with France, and lent her fleet to crush the power of the Dutch. Town after town was taken by the French, and the Dutch were in a terrible plight.

Young as he was, William carried on the war like an experienced general. His army had reverses at first; but his belief in the final triumph of the Dutch never left him.

Once a despondent official said to him, "Do you not see that the country is lost?"

"Lost!" replied William, "No, it is not lost; and I shall never see it lost!"

In this spirit of confidence he fought his enemies, never despairing, never acknowledging defeat.

After many successes the French were about to seize the city of Amsterdam. William ordered the dikes to be cut, and the waters of the North Sea spread over the lowlands. The growing crops were ruined, but the flood checked the invading army.

When, in 1674, peace was made with England, New York, which was originally a Dutch settlement and was called New Amsterdam, was ceded to Great Britain. It was renamed New York in honor of James, Duke of York, to whom his brother Charles II had, in 1664, granted all the land between the Connecticut and the Delaware.

France inflicted great disasters upon the Netherlands and actually secured part of her territory, but Louis was at length forced to withdraw from the country. The Dutch, under the heroic leadership of their young stadtholder, maintained their independence.

On the death of King Charles II, in 1685, the Duke of York came to the English throne under the title of James II.

He, however, aroused very great dissatisfaction in England by some of his acts; and in June 1688 a letter was sent to William of Orange, inviting him and his wife Mary, who was a daughter of James II., to become sovereigns of England.

This letter was signed by seven leading men of both the great political parties in England. It assured William that it was the universal wish of the English nation that he should become its ruler.

The invitation was accepted. The Netherlands, glad to have their honored stadtholder on the English throne, furnished him with an army of about thirteen thousand men, and a fleet of more than six hundred ships, and with these forces he reached England in November, 1688.

William landed his army and marched to Exeter, where the citizens welcomed him in a very enthusiastic manner. Thousands of the nobles, gentry and common people flocked to his standard. His army rapidly increased. Everywhere in England there was great rejoicing at his arrival.

King James gathered a strong force, mostly from Scotland and Ireland, and marched to Salisbury to check the revolt. But William met him bravely, and the king's army fell back in disorder and many of the officers and men deserted.

James gave up the struggle in despair, and hastened to London. There he learned that his daughter, Anne, had left his palace to join the revolters.

"God help me," cried the king, "for my own children have forsaken me!"

Coronation of William And Mary

His spirit was utterly broken, and he prepared for a rapid journey to France. He knew that the throne was lost to him, and he resolved to flee from England and cast himself upon the hospitality of his cousin, the French king, Louis XIV.

Leaving the palace at night, and in disguise, he threw the seals of state into the Thames, and then took a boat to a ship which was lying some distance down the river. James hoped to sail in this ship to France; but his escape was prevented by a fisherman who thought him a suspicious character, and he was brought back to London.

William and Mary, with the army that supported them, came to London. There was a wonderful demonstration of joy by the people of the metropolis, and the queen was greeted with acclamation. A committee of Parliament drew up a Declaration of Rights, which was presented to William and Mary. It declared what the rights of Englishmen are, stated that no sovereign could interfere with those rights, and expressed the resolve of both houses of Parliament to maintain them.

It seemed like a second Magna Charta. William and Mary both signed it, and they were then, in February, 1689, declared king and queen of England.

This change in the rulers—the abdication of King James and the coming of William and Mary—is called the Revolution of 1688.

As has been said, it was easily accomplished in England; but in Ireland there was decided opposition to it. Londonderry and Enniskillen were the only Irish towns that declared for William and Mary. The other towns were strongly in favor of James.

Finally, James came from France to Ireland, collected an army and began a war on those who supported the new sovereigns. He received assistance from Louis XIV of France. Those who fought for James were called "Jacobites" and the others were called "Orangemen." The war in Ireland lasted but a few months; for at the battle of the Boyne, on July 12, 1690, James's army was defeated, and all resistance in Ireland came to an end.

William was then formally recognized as king of Great Britain and Ireland.

England had declared war on France; and it became necessary for William to visit the European continent. He there made alliances with Austria, Spain, and other nations. While he was absent from England, Mary ruled the kingdom, and ruled it well.

Battle of La Hogue

William was engaged for some years in the contest on the continent. He won many great battles, but he also suffered disastrous defeats. While he was in Europe another attempt was made by James to invade England and regain the throne.

Louis XIV again provided James with soldiers and war ships; and an expedition sailed for England. James was confident of success; and all associated with him thought it would be an easy matter to accomplish the undertaking.

Near the coast of Normandy the invading fleet came upon the combined English and Dutch fleet; and, off Cape La Hogue, a furious battle took place. The English and Dutch gained a brilliant victory, and James sailed back to France, and never again made a movement to recover the English throne.

While England and France were fighting in Europe, the colonies of the two countries were fighting in America. The war is known in American history as King William's War.

The reign of William and Mary is of great interest to us in the United States. Those sovereigns were not accepted by the people of England until they had signed the Declaration of Rights; and the very first Act passed by Parliament during their reign was one which made the Declaration a part of the laws of the land.

That Declaration secured their rights not only to the subjects who lived in the "mother country," but also to those in the colonies. One of its provisions was "that it is the right of the subjects to petition the king."

George III spurned the petitions of the colonists, and otherwise violated the rights claimed in the Declaration, just as James II had done. What the American colonists did, therefore, when they fought the battles of the Revolution, was very similar to what the people of England had done a hundred years before, when they dethroned James and offered the crown to William and Mary.

The English Revolution of 1688, and the American Revolution, had exactly the same purpose.

CHAPTER 19

Sobieski

(1624-1694)

THE POLES first appeared in history in the fifth century under the name of Poliani.

There appears to have been a definitely organized kingdom of Poland as early as the tenth century. But the country did not rise into much prominence until the fourteenth century; and it attained its greatest splendor in the seventeenth.

The name Poland is derived from a word meaning plains. For many centuries great herds of cattle, horses, and swine have been raised within its territory; and cereals, hemp, timber, honey, and wax have been produced in large quantities.

Numerous mines of salt, and a few of iron, copper and silver, have been worked at different periods; but they are not of much value.

After passing through a vast number of changes, Poland became, in 1572, an elective monarchy; and this principal became one of the chief causes of the national downfall.

The nation consisted of but two classes, the nobles who owned the soil, and the serfs who cultivated it. There was no third estate.

At the time of which we write the Turks were at the height of their power in southeastern Europe. Their flag still waved, as it had done for a hundred and fifty years, over Belgrade; and Belgrade was the gateway to Hungary.

Their fleets swept the Mediterranean. They captured the island of Crete from the powerful state of Venice; and they fortified the Dardanelles, so that no ships could enter the Black Sea without their permission.

Poland being famous for its wheat and cattle, the Turks greatly desired to possess it.

They therefore invaded Poland with a large army; but the Poles met them bravely and in a great battle in which Sobieski served as commander-in-chief of the Polish forces succeeded in beating them back.

Just at that time the king of Poland died quite suddenly; and the Diet assembled to select a successor. Sobieski entered the hall where the Diet was in session and proposed the name of a French prince. Then one of the nobles was heard to say, "Let a Pole rule Poland." Sobieski was at once proposed and elected with hardly a dissentient voice.

Starhemberg, The Defender of Vienna

John Sobieski was born in 1624, at Olesko, in Galicia. His father was castellan or keeper of the castle of Cracow. John received an excellent education, both at home and in foreign countries; and this was of great advantage to him when he was elevated to the throne.

Poland was, at that time, one of the most powerful countries of Europe. It was stronger by far than Russia; and gave promise of a still greater future.

A hundred years before this the Turks had threatened Vienna, and they now determined to conquer all Austria.

In 1683 they gathered a vast army and marched a second time against Vienna, which was at that time not only the principal city of Austria, but the capital of the German Empire.

The emperor then ruling over Germany was Leopold I. He wore the crown of Charlemagne, but he was not worthy to do so.

As soon as he heard that the Turks were marching toward Vienna he fled from the city; and many of the nobles and wealthy people followed his example.

Count Starhemberg who was in command of the garrison stayed at his post, and did everything possible to prevent the city from falling into the hands of the enemy.

The fortifications needed repair. Not only the men but the women aided in the work. The women mixed mortar and even carried stone while the men built up the walls.

One day, as the people of Vienna were looking eastward, they saw columns of smoke ascending. Crops were burning, and houses and villages were in flames.

This told them, only too plainly, that the Turks were approaching; and at sunrise, on the fourteenth of July, 1683, they appeared before the city walls.

Their camp made a semicircle or crescent reaching more than half around the city.

As in Athens, during the terrible siege by the Spartans in the Peloponnesian War, so now in Vienna the plague broke out. This was because the people who had rushed into the city from the country were huddled so closely together.

The amount of sickness was terrible. Then a fire broke out; and as there were no fire engines nor other appliances with which to fight the flames, a great many houses were burned, and hundreds of families were rendered homeless. Things looked very discouraging; but just when they were at the worst help came.

Relief of Vienna

John Sobieski, king of Poland, was marching to the relief of the beleaguered city. He had sixty-five thousand men in his army; and John George, the Elector of Saxony had joined him with thirteen thousand more.

Before beginning the attack on the Turks, Sobieski made a speech to his men in which he said, "Not Vienna alone, but Christendom looks to you to-day. Not for an earthly sovereign do you fight. You are soldiers of the King of kings."

The battle cry was Sobieski's own name. It was well known to the Turks, for they had met him before, and thousands of Turks fled before hundreds of his Poles. His very name seemed to fill them with dread.

Large numbers of the Turkish soldiers stood their ground, however, and fought desperately; but they could not withstand the furious charges of the Poles.

Sobieski himself went into the battle singing the words of the psalm beginning: "Not unto us, O Lord, not unto us, but unto thy name give glory, for thy mercy, and for thy truth's sake."

Six of the sultan's pashas, or generals, were killed; and the grand vizier, or prime minister of Turkey, abandoned his splendid green silk tent that was embroidered with gold and silver, and fled for his life.

The whole Moslem army was routed; and the conqueror and his troops entered the city in triumph. A great service of thanksgiving was held in the cathedral; and one of the priests preached a sermon from the text: "There was a man sent from God whose name was John."

Never again did the Turks attack Vienna. City after city was lost to their empire; and all Hungary was finally won back from them.

Since Sobieski's great victory, the power of the Turks has steadily waned rather than increased.

They have been slowly pushed to the eastward until there is now little of value left to them in Europe but Constantinople.

The reign of John Sobieski was the most brilliant in Polish history. But the constant dissensions and the unending turbulence of the Polish nobles frustrated all his efforts to strengthen the kingdom, and prepared the way for its final dismemberment and ruin.

The hero of Poland has not, like Hercules and Perseus, given his name to a great constellation; but in the brightest part of the Milky Way hangs a gleaming expanse of star dust known as Sobieski's shield; so that, until the stars forget to shine, or men to watch them, the name of the great Polish hero will never be forgotten.

CHAPTER 20

Peter the Great

(1672–1725)

IN the history of Russia there is no name more famous than that of Peter the Great.

Before his time the Russians were far behind the other nations of Europe in knowledge of the arts and the comforts of life.

Peter devoted a large part of his reign to improving the condition of his country and his people. He made Russia prosperous, powerful, and respected.

He was born in 1672, and was the son of the Emperor Alexis. When only ten years old he came to the throne, together with his brother Ivan, who was almost an idiot. The boys were proclaimed joint emperors of Russia; but their sister, Sophia, who was many years older than they, acted as regent.

Sophia determined to make herself empress, and leagued herself with Galitzin, the prime minister, with that end in view.

"Madam," said Galitzin, "we need fear nothing from Ivan, but Peter alarms me. He has a thirst for knowledge that cannot be quenched. He wishes to know everything."

It was as the minister said. Peter had a remarkable desire for knowledge; and he learned many useful things.

When he was about seventeen years of age he was informed that his sister Sophia and Prince Galitzin intended to murder him. Peter at once banished Galitzin to the icy region of Archangel and confined his sister in a convent. He thus became, at about eighteen years of age, the active ruler of Russia; for Ivan could take no share in the government.

Peter the Great

Peter listened to others before taking important action. He valued particularly the advice of a brilliant Swiss, named Lefort, to whom he gave a high position in his court.

Lefort urged that the army should be made larger, and be better drilled and equipped. The young emperor accepted this advice. He appointed Lefort to be commander of one division of his army, and directed him to equip and drill it in the very best manner.

Peter himself served for a few months under the command of Lefort as a common soldier. He performed all his duties with the greatest faithfulness. He became a subordinate officer, and then rose gradually through every grade until he reached the rank of general.

Under Lefort's direction the army was made a splendid body of fighting men.

One day, in the early part of his reign, Peter noticed on the river which flows through Moscow a small boat with a keel. He inquired what the keel was for, and was greatly interested to learn that it was to enable the boat to sail against the wind.

The boat had been built for Peter's father by a Dutchman named Brandt; and this man was at once instructed to put it into first-rate order. This being done, the Dutchman gave Peter some lessons in sailing, so that the young czar became quite an expert sailor.

Russia at that time had only one seaport. It was Archangel on the White Sea. So to Archangel the czar went, and made it his home for several months.

While there, he made the acquaintance of a Dutch captain named Musch; and from him he learned all about ships and their management. He began as a cabin boy, and worked up through every department of a seafaring life until he was fitted to be a naval commander.

Peter the Great as a Shipwright in Holland

Peter felt that he must have a navy and must be at its head; so he thought he ought to know about the building of ships as well as their management. He therefore determined to go to Holland and learn the art of shipbuilding.

Putting the affairs of his empire in charge of three nobles, he left Russia, with Lefort and some other companions, and went to Amsterdam, the most important city of the Netherlands.

After visiting Amsterdam and examining its shipping and its docks, he went to a little town called Zaandam nearby, and there became a workman in a yard where ships were built for the famous Dutch East India Company. He lived in a little cottage near the yard and cooked his own food.

After working some time in Zaandam he spent four or five months as a shipwright near London, because some things connected with shipbuilding could be better learned in England than in the Netherlands.

When, by taking lessons in both countries, he had thoroughly mastered the art, he returned to his own country.

He now began the building of the Russian navy at a place in southern Russia, on the Verona River. The vessels built were small gunboats.

While they were being built, someone said to Peter, "Of what use will your vessels be to you? You have no good seaport."

"My vessels shall make ports for themselves," replied Peter; and before long they did so.

The first port captured was Azof at the mouth of the Don. It was taken from the Turks. The Russian fleet sailed down the river, and made the attack by sea; while twelve thousand troops attacked by land. Peter himself was sometimes with the army on land, sometimes on board one of his vessels.

The capture of Azof gave Russia a port on the Black Sea. But this was only the beginning. A greater work was done in the north, at the mouth of the Neva.

When Peter came to the throne, Sweden was the great military and naval power of northern Europe. The Swedes were masters of the Baltic Sea, and of the Gulf of Finland. Peter said that the Swedes were the oppressors of Russia; and that he would free the land from their presence.

When in the Netherlands he had lived near Amsterdam. It was a great seaport near the mouth of a river. The land upon which it stood was swampy; and its dwellings, its warehouses, and its magnificent churches and public buildings rested on piles.

The River Neva flows into the Gulf of Finland. Peter determined to build a Russian Amsterdam on its swampy banks.

The king of Sweden, the famous Charles XII, claimed the province at the mouth of the River Neva. In spite of this Peter laid the foundations of his new city and called it St. Petersburg.

When the king of Sweden heard what was going on he said, "I shall soon put those houses into a blaze."

The Swedish fortresses guarded the province and the mouth of the river. Whoever held them would control the commerce of St. Petersburg.

The Swedish king was astonished soon after hearing that the foundations of St. Petersburg had been laid, to learn that Peter's new army and navy had captured his two fortresses, and that the province at the mount of the Neva was in Peter's hands.

Soon afterward, with a well drilled army, Charles laid siege to Poltava, a small fortified town of the Russians. Peter marched against him. Both sovereigns commanded their armies in person.

Charles had been wounded in his heel, and had to be carried into battle on a litter. During the battle a cannon-ball killed one of the bearers and shattered the litter; whereupon the king is said to have ordered some of the men to carry him upon their pikes.

Peter, like Charles, was in the hottest of the fire. His clothes were shot through in several places, one ball going through his hat.

After desperate fighting on both sides the Swedes gave way. They left more than half their number dead or wounded upon the field.

Only a few hundred men escaped with the king who, it is said, was taken off the field in a carriage drawn by twelve horses.

The victory at Poltava was followed by naval successes in the Gulf of Finland. Abo, then the capital of Finland, and Helsingfors, which is the present capital, were both captured, and the Russians became masters of the gulf.

Peter was determined that his people should become a commercial nation. He urged them to engage in foreign trade and encouraged foreigners to bring their merchandise to Russia's new ports. Less than six months after the first stone of St. Petersburg was laid, a large ship under Dutch colors ascended the Neva and anchored off the city site.

Peter himself went on board to welcome the strangers. The skipper was invited to dine at the house of one of the nobles. Peter and several officers of his government bought the entire cargo; and when the ship sailed from St. Petersburg the captain received a present of about two hundred dollars, and each of his crew a smaller sum of money, as a premium for having brought the first foreign vessel into the new port.

Peter encouraged his people in the different parts of Russia to carry on commerce with one another, and he made it easy for them to do so. He improved the roads, aided in providing boats for navigating the rivers, and undertook the gigantic work of uniting the great seas, the Baltic, the Black and the Caspian Seas by canals.

Toward the close of his reign Peter visited the town of Zaandam in Holland where he had learned the trade of shipbuilding. There he found some of his old companions, and was delighted to hear them salute him as Peter Bass, the name by which they had known him nearly twenty years before.

He went to the little cottage in which he had lived. It is still carefully preserved. In one room are to be seen the little oak table and three chairs which were there when Peter occupied it. Over the chimney-piece is an inscription which every boy who is making his way up in the world might well take for his motto, "To a great man nothing is little."

Peter went to see an old friend, Kist the blacksmith, who was at work in his smithy. The czar took the job from him. He blew the bellows, heated the piece of iron and beat it out with the great hammer into the required shape. Though he was the ruler of millions of people he was proud of being a workman and of being able to do things for himself.

No sovereign ever more truly deserved the title "Great" than did Peter. He found his empire feeble and left it with a well-drilled army and a large navy. He found it without commerce. He secured for it ports to which foreign ships might bring merchandise; and he dug canals so that the different parts of the country might easily carry on trade with one another.

Thus he was, in the best sense, great, because he made his country great; and provided for his people new and better ways of living.

CHAPTER 21

Charles XII

(1682-1718)

IN the year 1697 a strange coronation service took place in the city of Stockholm. A boy of only fifteen years of age was crowned king of Sweden, and took the title of Charles XII.

He was born in 1682. When he was only three or four years old the queen went into the nursery to take him to church, but he refused to get down from the high chair in which he was perched because he had promised his nurse that he would not leave his seat until she had given him permission.

He was taught German as well as Swedish as soon as he could speak; and history, geography, and arithmetic seemed like play to him.

When only four years old he was put astride a horse, and at eight he was a good rider. At eleven he killed his first bear; and before he was twelve he shot a stag at a distance of ninety yards.

As soon as he began to wear the crown he became very pompous and arrogant. No one was allowed to find fault with anything that he did.

About a year after Charles was made king two princesses were brought to Stockholm to spend the winter in the hope that he would marry one of them.

But Charles did not marry either of them. In fact he was never really in love with anybody or with anything but war.

One day, when he was out on a bear hunt, news was brought to him that the kings of Denmark and Poland, and Peter the Great of Russia, had formed a combination against him, and proposed to capture Sweden and divide it among themselves.

He gathered an army, placed himself at its head, sailed for Denmark and soon forced the Danes to sue for peace.

He then marched against the Russians. The Russians were five times as many as the Swedes, but Charles said, "With my brave boys in blue behind me I am afraid of nothing."

On the march four hundred Swedes had been attacked by six thousand Russians; but the Swedes had beaten them off. Peter the Great and his men ran away as soon as the Swedes approached.

But Charles followed them and a great battle was fought in a driving snow storm. Charles lost one of his boots in a bog, and a bullet was flattened against his clothing; but by nightfall the Swedes had won a complete victory. Charles was then only eighteen years of age.

The next summer the young warrior marched against the united armies of Russia and Poland. After a fight which lasted all day Charles was again victorious.

Among the ladies of Poland was the beautiful Marie Aurora. She wrote a letter to Charles asking that she might see him, in the hope of ending the war; but Charles made no reply.

Then Aurora traveled to the Swedish camp, although it was the depth of winter; but the king refused to see her.

The lady, however, was not discouraged. One day she saw him riding toward her, and at once got out of her carriage and knelt before him in the muddy road. Charles raised his hat and made a low bow; but, without stopping, he put spurs to his horse and went off at a gallop. In about three weeks both the capitals of Poland—Warsaw and Cracow—were in his hands.

Charles at once found work for his army elsewhere. Saxony which then belonged to his great enemy Augustus was invaded and captured; and Charles remained in possession of it for more than a year.

While Charles was busy with Saxony, Peter the Great attacked his provinces on the Baltic. He took possession of the principal ports, and founded on Swedish territory his new capital, St. Petersburg.

In the defense of his territories, Charles engaged in several fierce battles with the Russians and finally defeated them.

The Russians retreated and burned all the bridges behind them.

He next determined to go to the succor of the Cossacks of the Ukraine. It was December. The cold was so intense that the Baltic Sea was frozen over, and many of the birds fell dead from the trees. The Swedes were poorly clothed, and they suffered greatly from the cold. Over three thousand were frozen to death, and many others were frost-bitten.

Charles had lost twenty thousand out of an army of forty-one thousand. Yet he would not give up the struggle, but determined to lay siege to the fortress of Poltava.

Up to this time Charles had seemed to bear a charmed life. But one day a bullet struck his foot. Some of the small bones were broken, and the flesh had to be cut open to remove the splinters. Charles watched the operation without flinching; but the wound gave him trouble, and he had to be carried about in a litter, as we have read in the story of Peter the Great.

The "boys in blue" did wonders, but the struggle was really hopeless. They were utterly defeated, and Charles barely escaped with his life.

He at length crossed the River Dnieper with the remnant of his army and took refuge with the Turks; and in the Turkish town of Bender, seven hundred miles from Sweden, he lived for several years.

The sultan of Turkey treated him kindly, and in Bender, Charles built for himself a stone house with walls like those of a fort.

The sultan also gave him a bodyguard of janissaries. These men became very fond of him and when they found what a strong will he had, they called him "Iron Head." Some of them said, "If Allah (God) would only give us such a ruler we could conquer the world."

Peter the Great had seized certain Turkish ports on the Black Sea, as well as the Swedish ports of the Baltic. So Charles proposed to the sultan that the Turks and Swedes should unite their forces against Russia. To this the sultan agreed and, in 1710, war was declared and an army of two hundred thousand men marched against the Russians.

Peter had only about forty thousand, and he was very anxious for peace. He sent a wagonload of money to the Turkish commander and persuaded him to sign a treaty.

Charles was not with the Turkish army when this was done; but he arrived immediately afterwards. He was terribly disappointed, and more so when the sultan wrote him a letter advising him to return to Sweden.

Charles refused to go. This made the sultan angry; and he sent orders to seize Charles and take him, alive or dead, away from Bender.

Charles sent word back that if they attempted to do this he would fight; and so an attack was made upon him in the house which he had built as a defense.

Some of the Turkish soldiers refused to fight against him, and thirty of them were drowned in the River Dnieper by the sultan's orders.

Fifty of the soldiers who were friendly to him tried to persuade Charles to put himself into their hands; and when they failed they said, "Oh, Iron Head! Allah has made thee mad!"

Twelve thousand Turks then attacked Charles in his quarters. He fought bravely for his life, but was finally captured and turned over to the Turkish commander.

He looked very unlike a king. His clothes were torn to rags, and his face was so blackened with powder and smeared with blood that he could scarcely be recognized.

When the people in Sweden heard of his capture some were greatly delighted at the king's bravery; but the wisest men of the kingdom felt grieved; and, all over Europe, it was said that Charles had gone mad.

Some of the people in Sweden now said that unless Charles returned to Sweden they must have another ruler; and a letter was sent to him imploring him to come home.

This caused him at last to leave Turkey; and at midnight, of November 11, 1714, he entered the fortified town of Stralsund, which belonged to Sweden. His people were overjoyed at his return, but were disappointed that he did not cross the Baltic and come into Sweden itself.

The neighboring powers were glad to have him stay in Stralsund. Six of them—Russia, Prussia, Poland, Saxony, Denmark and Hanover—had declared war against Sweden; and they thought they could capture King Charles quite easily while he was in Stralsund.

They besieged the town; but Charles defended it bravely. To encourage his men he went to the most dangerous places. He even took his meals within range of the enemy's guns. He slept on the ground with a stone for his pillow; and shared all the hardships of the siege equally with the common soldiers.

But, in spite of all his bravery, Charles saw that Stralsund must surrender. He therefore crossed the Baltic in a boat and made his home in the city of Lund, in Sweden. Poor Sweden was almost ruined; and its future looked very dark indeed. It seemed as though Charles could not see in what a wretched state his kingdom was.

Charles XII Defends His House Against the Turks

Everybody else knew that Sweden must have peace; for she had lost in battle or by disease almost one fourth of all her men.

Most of the fisheries were abandoned, because the fishermen had been taken to man the fleet. A large part of the farms were cultivated by women and boys. There was a great scarcity of meat, butter, and tallow; and as tallow was used for making candles, the people were unable to work in the mornings or evenings, because no candles could be bought.

The king shared the poverty of his people. There was no silver on his table. All his dishes were of pewter. He slept on a straw mattress with his cloak spread over him.

His passion for war was as strong as ever; and finally he determined to invade Norway, which then belonged to Denmark.

He attacked the Norwegian fortress called Fredericksten. Trenches were dug within gunshot of the fortress. One morning as he was looking over the top of one of the trenches, he was struck by a bullet and instantly killed.

Charles was a brave man, but he was not a good ruler. He had a great fondness for fighting, and a strange power of making others fond of it. His people loved him; and they continue to honor him. He brought his country to the verge of ruin. More than one hundred and fifty thousand men perished in his wars; and he left Sweden poorer both in territory and in wealth than it was when his reign began.

CHAPTER 22

Frederick the Great

(1712-1786)

IN the year 1730 all Europe was startled with strange news. Tidings went from kingdom to kingdom that the crown prince of Prussia had been condemned to death by a court martial on a charge brought by his father the king.

When the news reached Vienna, the emperor of Austria sent word to the Prussian king begging him not to allow his son to be executed, and the kings of Poland and Sweden made the same request.

The young man was charged with being a deserter from the Prussian army. He belonged to a famous regiment called the "Potsdam Guard," of which his father was very proud.

His father was a hard, harsh man. The one thing that he loved to do was to save money—the one thing that he disliked to do was to spend it.

Frederick had been made to study hard when he was only seven years old. His father's rule was that he should get up at six in the morning, not staying in bed one minute after he was called.

On Saturday morning he was examined on the lessons learned during the week, and if he passed a good examination, the afternoon was given him as a half holiday; if the examination was not good, he had to stay in and study.

Then besides studying he was obliged before he was twelve years old to drill as a soldier. But young Frederick was not so fond of playing soldier as most boys are.

You will not be surprised to hear that the crown prince was not very fond of his father, and the king seems to have really hated the prince. Once it is said that he tried to strangle him to death with the cord of a curtain.

The prince at length made up his mind that he would run away from his father's palace and go to stay with his uncle, George II, who was king of England. But his father discovered his plan and thwarted it.

Frederick the Great

Then came the court martial. The prince was found guilty of deserting his regiment, and was sentenced to death. He would have been executed had not the emperor of Austria and the kings of Poland and Sweden said so much against it.

A few days later the prince signed a promise to submit to his father. He was then released from prison and watched very carefully. As he now behaved himself to suit the crusty old king, he was made colonel of the Potsdam Guard.

Not long after this his father had a serious sickness, and was never quite strong again as long as he lived. He became softened and affectionate toward his son, and before his death he saw what a mistake he had made in thinking so little of him.

Frederick II began his reign on May 31, 1740. The next day he made this promise to the people, "Our great care shall be to make every one of our subjects contented and happy."

He began well. Sometime before his father's death, the crops in Prussia had failed, and a famine prevailed; but the miserly old king was afraid of being cheated and would not sell to the people the wheat which belonged to the crown. Frederick II at once sold the grain to all who needed it, and ordered that a thousand poor women should be comfortably fed and clothed at his own expense.

He altered his manner of living. He made a great change in the army, enlarged it to the number of one hundred thousand, and, very early in his reign, he went to war.

His reason for fighting was this. About a hundred years before he was born one of his ancestors made an agreement with the duke of a province called Silesia, that if either of them should die without an heir, his territory should go to the other.

This agreement was duly written on parchment and signed and sealed. The Duke of Silesia died leaving no heir. So, by the agreement, Silesia ought to have become part of Prussia. However, the archduke of Austria took possession of it. It had been a part of Austria so long that most people seemed to have forgotten that Prussia had a claim to it.

Frederick II did not forget; and soon after he came to the throne he wrote to Maria Theresa, the archduchess of Austria, and made the claim that Silesia was part of his dominions. He offered to pay a large sum of money for the province, though he said it was his; but Maria refused to give it or sell it.

Frederick without loss of time marched with a large army into the country. Breslau, the capital of Silesia, opened its gates to him without resistance, and most of the other towns followed its example.

Maria Theresa sent a large army into the field, and Frederick's first battle was fought. It took place near a town called Mollwitz. This battle is famous not because of the number of men who were killed and wounded, but because King Frederick himself fled from the field. After his flight the tide turned, and his troops gained the victory.

Maria Theresa was greatly alarmed. But she did a very wise thing. She was queen of Hungary as well as archduchess of Austria. She knew that the Hungarians were great fighters. So she invited the nobles of Hungary to meet her, and said to them, "You are my only allies, and I throw myself on your generosity." These words went to their hearts and they voted that all Hungary should arm and fight for her.

But her troops were again badly defeated and she was forced to surrender nearly all of Silesia to Frederick. In twenty months Frederick thus won for Prussia a territory larger than Massachusetts, Connecticut, and Rhode Island put together.

And really it was a fortunate thing for the Silesians that they became Prussians. The province was soon far more productive and prosperous than it had ever been, and the people were a great deal happier.

When peace came, Frederick was as busy at home as on the field of battle. To do what he thought a king ought to do, he found that his day must contain a great many hours. So he gave orders that a servant should awaken him at four o'clock.

On several mornings he dropped asleep again after being called. So he ordered the servant to mop his face at four o'clock with a cold wet towel. This made him wide awake, and through his life, four was his hour for rising. He went to bed about nine or ten; so he hardly ever had more than six hours sleep.

Maria Theresa kept him busy, for she did not rest content with the loss of Silesia. Frederick had reason to suppose that she was going to try to regain the lost province; so he immediately invaded her territories. He gained four victories, and thus secured Silesia a second time.

After Frederick had conquered her in the second Silesian War, she found Russia, France, Sweden, and Saxony ready to fight against him.

The Justice of Frederick

Frederick Addressing His Generals

Maria Theresa and her new friends agreed that they would destroy Frederick's army, get possession of Prussia, and divide it among themselves.

But Frederick took his enemies by surprise. On August 24, 1756, he invaded Saxony, and thus began what is known as the Seven Years' War.

At the very beginning he was successful and forced the whole Saxon army to surrender. After this, however, his good fortune left him. The Austrians gained a great victory over him at a place called Kolin (ko len'); and in about three years from the beginning of the war the allies had really almost ruined him.

Another great battle was fought with the Austrians and Prussians at a place called Kunersdorf (koo' ners dorf). When Frederick saw that this battle also was likely to be lost, he led the attack three times himself. Three horses were killed under him. A bullet struck a small metal box in his vest pocket and was flattened. Had it not been for the box he must have been killed.

All his efforts, however, were in vain. The defeat was terrible, and Frederick was in despair. He wrote to a friend, "All is lost. I will not survive the ruin of the Fatherland. Adieu forever." It is said at this time he kept in his pocket some little pills of poison ready to take, if all seemed hopeless.

Then a piece of good luck happened. The Russians expected the Austrians to feed their army because it was fighting for them; but, instead of sending flour, the Austrians sent money. The Russian general said that his men could not eat silver; and as winter was approaching, he marched home to Russia.

The campaign of the year now closing, 1759, the year so famous in America for the conquest of Canada by the English—had been most unfortunate for Frederick. He had lost six thousand men, and Prussia was nearly exhausted both of men and of money.

But the king was wonderfully brave, and he inspired all Prussia with courage and hope. Besides, he gained some victories. One night when he was sitting half asleep by one of his watch fires, a horseman galloped into camp, exclaiming, "Where is the king?"

"Here!" answered Frederick.

The rider hurriedly said, "The enemy has driven in our outposts and is not five hundred yards from our left wing."

Instantly Frederick gave his orders, and in a few minutes ten cannons were pouring shot into the ranks of the enemy. The attack of the Austrians was terrible; but the Prussians stood their ground heroically, and the Austrians were driven back. They lost ten thousand men, the Prussians only eighteen hundred.

The tide had turned, and another great battle gained at Torgau (tor'gou) left Frederick a third time master of Silesia. When a treaty was made, Maria Theresa was obliged to give up the province forever.

Prussia at the beginning of Frederick's reign had been small and insignificant. At the end of the Seven Years' War she was one of the great powers of Europe.

Frederick was as great in peace as in war. He lent money to those in need. He furnished seed to the farmers. He called himself "the chief servant of the state," and really worked like a slave for the good of his people. It is said that in seven years the country was as prosperous as ever.

One of the most remarkable and one of the saddest things ever done in Europe was what is called the "Partition of Poland." Russia, Austria, and Prussia determined to cut up the little kingdom and divide it among themselves.

Yet Prussia's share of Poland was much benefited by being brought under the government of Frederick. When he took charge of it the people were in a wretched condition. Frederick soon changed all this and the country became prosperous and its inhabitants comfortable.

To the last he was a rigid disciplinarian; he was as severe upon himself as upon others. In August, 1786, he ordered the army to go through a number of sham fights. While witnessing one of these he caught a chill which brought on an illness from which he never recovered.

At about twelve o'clock on the night of his death, one of his dogs which was sitting near him was shivering with cold, and Frederick said "Throw a quilt over him." These were the last words which he spoke, and at half past two he was dead.

CHAPTER 23

William Pitt

(1708-1778)

WHILE Frederick the Great was making Prussia a prominent European power, the elder William Pitt, first Earl of Chatham, was making England great.

He held the office of prime minister only once, and that for not more than two years; but his wisdom and uprightness gave him such influence that he was the real ruler of the country for many years.

He was born in 1708, in the southwestern part of England, his father being a country gentleman of prominent family and considerable wealth.

The childhood of the future statesman was passed amid rural scenes and pleasures. As a boy he was remarkably fond of books; and by his careful attention to study he gratified both his parents and his teachers.

He was also a lover of sports and games. This, however, did not prevent his suffering, even during his school days, from attack of gout, a disease which he inherited.

When he entered Trinity College, Oxford, few students of his age were so well-read. But owing to his lack of robust health he was obliged to leave the university, without taking his degree. Going to the continent, he spent two years in travel and study in France and Italy. He then returned to England, and secured an officer's commission in a regiment of dragoons.

He soon discovered that he had made a mistake in choosing the army as a profession. He saw that his best work could be done in public life.

William Pitt

The young officer immediately began to take steps to secure a public position. Fortunately, the right of representing the borough of Old Sarum belonged to his family, and thus he was enabled to become a member of Parliament.

His speeches in the House of Commons were forcible and at times very eloquent. One day he spoke against a measure proposed by Horace Walpole, then prime minister of England. Walpole was so offended at the strong language of Pitt that he had the latter dismissed from the army, with which he had not as yet severed his connection.

"Now I shall turn my energies wholly to politics," Pitt said to his friends. "I am really glad Walpole has prevented my remaining in the army. I am not in any way fitted to be a soldier."

From the time that Pitt entered Parliament to the last day of his life he was devoted to public affairs. He quickly showed that he had great genius for political management.

There was no orator in the House of Commons whose speeches commanded so much attention. But the source of his power was no mystery. It was the simple fact that he invariably advocated measures which he believed to be for the benefit of the people.

After some experience in political life he was chosen a member of the Cabinet, and though he was not nominally prime minister, he was really at the head of the government. Nearly all its important measures were suggested by him.

He ventured, on one occasion, to oppose the wishes of King George II, and consequently was obliged to resign his position. But the king found it impossible to carry on the government without him. The people demanded that he should return to office, and within a few months he was recalled.

The condition of England at this time was one of feebleness. Pitt put the army and navy into such a condition that during the famous "Seven Years' War" in which England, as the ally of Frederick the Great, was at war with France, the latter country was forced to cede to England most valuable possessions both in America and India.

Pitt inspired England with national enthusiasm. It was during the years 1756–1761 that he had the fullest opportunity to show his surpassing qualities. His wise choice of men like Wolfe in Canada and Clive in India, and his vigorous measures in the management of foreign affairs, made England respected in every part of the world.

The people called him the "great commoner," because, up to this time, he was without a title of nobility. Never before had so great a leader of public affairs appeared in England.

The young king was obstinate. He was determined to be "a real king," as he said. So one day when Pitt advised that war should be declared against Spain, which had made an alliance with France, the great enemy of England, the king and his council refused to agree to such a war. Pitt then decided to give up his office and have nothing further to do with the management of the government.

The king received his resignation calmly, and made no request to Pitt to remain in office; nevertheless, he granted him a pension of fifteen thousand dollars a year.

After his retirement from office, Pitt remained in the House of Commons; and was, as he had so long been, its foremost member. His eloquent voice was constantly heard in the debates, and his word had influence not only with Parliament, but with the whole nation.

The Death of William Pitt

Twice he was urged to take part in the government but refused. At last, in 1766, King George invited him to choose a ministry to suit himself, and Pitt accepted the invitation.

In the new ministry he selected for himself the office of Privy Seal, with a seat in the House of Lords as Viscount Pitt and Earl of Chatham. His acceptance of a title lost him at first considerable popularity; but his continued devotion to the people's interests, even as a member of the nobility, eventually restored public confidence.

He ceased to be prime minister in 1768 and was succeeded in that office by Lord North.

Like Burke, he denounced in the most fearless manner the arbitrary and unjust measures of the government of Lord North toward the American colonies. He insisted that the colonists were entitled to all the rights of British subjects; and urged in the warmest way that the difficulties between them and the government should be amicably settled.

The name of Pittsburg, in Pennsylvania, was given by his American admirers to commemorate his efforts in behalf of the rights of his colonial fellow citizens.

When he died, in May 1778, the entire English nation, in the colonies as well as at home, mourned with genuine grief. He had been a patriot and a statesman—not a mere politician.

CHAPTER 24

George Washington

(1732-1799)

GEORGE WASHINGTON, familiarly known as the Father of his Country, was born on a plantation in Virginia called Bridge's Creek, on February 22, 1732.

When he was three years old the house in which he was born was burned down, and the family moved to another plantation on the Rappahannock, opposite Fredericksburg.

He was the eldest of five children, although he had a half-brother named Lawrence, who was fifteen years older than himself.

His father died when he was but eleven years of age. But his mother, who was a strong and healthy woman, took up her burden bravely and brought up her family with great care.

It is generally admitted that Washington got his manly qualities from his mother. In features and in mental characteristics he resembled her very closely.

After the death of George's father one of his estates called Mount Vernon, on the Potomac River, was inherited by Lawrence.

Lawrence Washington was fond of George, and often invited him to spend his holidays at Mount Vernon.

An English nobleman, named Lord Fairfax, lived near Mount Vernon, and often visited Lawrence Washington. In this way he became acquainted with George. Lord Fairfax owned an immense tract of wild forest land in Virginia. He had never seen it himself, and few white men had ever been on it. Lord Fairfax was an old gentleman, but he took a great liking to George Washington.

When he found that the young man understood surveying, he engaged him to survey these lands.

When only sixteen George entered upon his task. This was quite an undertaking for one so young. But in three years the survey was finished; and it was so well done that it stands to this day.

Lawrence Washington died in 1752, and in his will he made George guardian to his daughter and heir to Mount Vernon in case of her death.

George had now grown to manhood. He was wonderfully strong and athletic and could out-run, out-leap and out-ride all the young men of his acquaintance.

So fully did he command the confidence of those who knew him that he was appointed to positions of great trust and responsibility.

At the age of twenty-three he was made colonel and commander-in-chief of all the forces raised in Virginia for the defense of the Western Territory against the French.

In this French War, as it was called, he received a splendid training, not only in success but in failure, and confidence in him was greatly increased when men saw how these failures and defeats raised his unconquerable spirit.

In a second expedition Washington was again placed in command of the American troops. The French had built a fort at the point where the Allegheny and Monongahela Rivers join and form the Ohio, which they called Fort Duquesne.

Washington decided to capture this fort; but the French garrisons were afraid to risk a battle; so they burned the fort and marched away into Canada.

When Washington and his men arrived they found nothing but smoking ruins; but they took possession of the place in the name of King George.

Sometime afterward, the English won a great victory over the French at Quebec. This gave them all French America from the St. Lawrence and the Great Lakes as far west as the Mississippi, and south to the Gulf of Mexico. At the end of the war, Washington returned to Mount Vernon.

In May, 1758, Washington was called to Williamsburg to confer with the governor in regard to the condition of the Virginia troops. He traveled there on horseback, accompanied by his servant; and one day he stopped for dinner at the mansion of a hospitable planter.

There he was introduced to a lovely young widow, Mrs. Martha Custis. Her manners and conversation were so pleasing to him that he spent the afternoon and evening in her company; and the next morning he rode away a captive to her charms.

Washington as a Surveyor

George Washington and Martha Custis were married on January 6, 1759. The union proved to be a very happy one. She adorned every station to which his greatness called her, and he was tenderly devoted to her till the end of his life.

For several years Washington lived the life of a country gentleman. He was very fond of horses and hounds and often went fox hunting. But like other people in the American colonies he was greatly troubled by the unjust way in which the English king and his government were acting.

The English Parliament ordered that a tax should be paid upon all the tea brought into New York, Boston, and the other ports of the colonies. As the colonists had no representative in Parliament they felt that they ought not to be taxed; and when a shipload of tea arrived in Boston a number of citizens went on board the vessel and threw the chests of tea into the harbor. This was called the "Boston Tea Party."

Washington hated the tea tax, and he and his friends refused to buy any goods that came from England. A number of men from all the colonies met together in a Congress to consider what should be done. They sent a letter to the king of England begging that they might have the same rights as those of his subjects who were born in England.

Signing the Declaration of Independence

Quite a number of men in the English Parliament said that the colonists were right. Among these was William Pitt, after whom the city of Pittsburg was named. But the Parliament was stubborn, and the Americans found that if they were to gain their rights they could only do so by fighting for them. So they took up arms and entered upon a great struggle for their liberties.

The Congress of the Colonies raised an army, and Washington was made commander-in-chief.

British troops had already been sent over to fight against the colonists. As Washington was riding from Mount Vernon to Cambridge, Massachusetts, people told him that a battle had taken place between the English soldiers and the colonial militia.

His question was, "Did the militia fight?"

"Yes!" was the answer.

"Then" said Washington, "the liberties of the country are safe."

On arriving at Cambridge, Washington at once assumed command. The British held the city of Boston, but Washington made up his mind to take it.

One cold night in March he fortified a hill which commanded the city. From its heights he discharged such a shower of shot and shell that the British commander found that Boston was not a safe place for him to stay in; so he took to his ships and left the city in Washington's hands.

This was a great victory for the colonists and they were much encouraged. On the fourth of July, 1776, Congress declared that the colonies no longer belonged to Great Britain, but were free and independent.

A British fleet and army now arrived from England to capture New York. They landed on Long Island, and a battle was fought in which the Americans were badly defeated.

The British rested for a couple of days after the battle; and during that time Washington led the American army across the East River, marched through New York, and on through Harlem to White Plains. There they dug trenches, threw up breastworks, and awaited the British attack.

The English commander hesitated to attack them in this strong position, and Washington soon afterward crossed the Hudson into New Jersey.

These were dark days for all who were fighting for liberty and independence. On several occasions Washington saved his army only by rapidly retreating from place to place.

At Christmas, 1777, the main body of the British army were in winter quarters at New York, and the towns of Princeton and Trenton, in New Jersey, were also, held by them. Washington determined to make an advance movement against them.

He crossed the Delaware amidst floating ice, marched to Trenton in a driving storm of sleet, and captured the town. He was also successful at Princeton, and Frederick the Great, the most famous soldier of Prussia, declared that

"Washington's victories at Trenton and Princeton were the most splendid gained in the eighteenth century."

Washington Crossing the Delaware

He next won a great battle at Monmouth in New Jersey, and after that the outlook began to improve.

Benjamin Franklin was then in Paris, and he persuaded the French government to help his countrymen. So a French fleet and an army came over, and rendered good service to the American cause.

The Marquis de Lafayette, a young French nobleman had already come to this country and joined the colonial army. Washington admired him very greatly, and made him a major general. He was a brave man and a brilliant soldier, and will ever be kindly remembered by the American people.

In 1781, the main division of the British army was at Yorktown in Virginia under the command of Lord Cornwallis.

As soon as the French allies arrived, Washington went to see the commander of the fleet; and it was agreed that the French and Americans should unite and make an attack on Cornwallis. The French fleet sailed to Yorktown; and the French and Americans closing in upon the town by land, it was soon besieged on all sides.

The British army was so closely cooped up in Yorktown that Cornwallis was finally obliged to surrender; and this victory brought the war to an end.

Peace was made with England, and Washington returned to his beautiful home at Mount Vernon where he would have liked to spend the rest of his life in quiet. But the country still needed his help.

Washington and Lafayette at Mount Vernon

Although our country was called the "United States of America" the states were not really united. They had joined in the war against England because all were in the same danger. But as soon as the danger was over, they began to disagree among themselves.

There were thirteen independent states. Each of these states had its own governor, but there was no president over all.

There was really no nation, and of course there was no constitution. Washington said there must be a union that would keep the states together in peace as well as in war.

Most of the people felt as he did; and so, in 1789, a constitution was drawn up and adopted by the states.

This constitution provided that there should be a president elected by the people to be the ruler of the nation; that laws should be made which the people in all the states must obey; and that these laws should be made by Congress and the president.

After the constitution had been adopted, an election was held, and George Washington, being the unanimous choice of his countrymen, became the first president of the United States of America.

New York was then the capital city of the country, and after his election Washington went to live there. His journey from Mount Vernon to New York was one long triumphal march.

Congress then held its meetings in a hall in Wall Street; and in front of that hall he took the oath to serve the country faithfully and to maintain the constitution.

An immense crowd had gathered to witness this ceremony; and as soon as it was performed they shouted "God bless George Washington, president of the United States." Bells pealed and cannons roared, and there was great rejoicing all over the land.

So well did Washington rule that when his term of office expired he was again the choice of the people; and they would have elected him a third time had not he himself declined the great honor.

He wrote "A Farewell Address to the People of the United States," and went back to Virginia to live amid the quiet scenes of Mount Vernon and enjoy a well-earned rest.

Not quite three years passed when, in December, 1799, he took a severe cold as he was riding over his farm in a storm of sleet. He failed very rapidly from the first; and, two days later, George Washington, the Father of his Country, was dead.

He was buried at Mount Vernon. The entire nation sincerely mourned the loss of its founder and friend; and the world grieved for the death of one of its grandest heroes.

Inaugeration of Washington

CHAPTER 25

Robespierre

(1758-1794)

A FEW years after the American Revolution had freed the thirteen colonies from the tyranny of George III, the great French Revolution began.

This was also a struggle against tyranny, and Americans can scarcely help sympathizing with the French who, for many generations, had been deprived of their just rights.

One of the great leaders of the French Revolution was Robespierre (robs pyar'). He was born at Arras, in France, on May 6, 1758. He was left an orphan at the age of nine and obtained his early education in the schools of his native town through the kindness of a warm-hearted bishop who had known his father.

He afterwards entered the college of Louis le Grand in Paris. He was a clever student, and when Louis XVI entered Paris, at the beginning of his reign, Robespierre was chosen by vote of his fellow students to present him with an address of welcome.

Robespierre

After his graduation, in 1781, he was called to the bar; but resigned on account of his reluctance to pronounce sentence of death. Nevertheless, it is said that he was cruel even as a child, and that he took great pleasure in mean little acts that would give pain to others.

He appears to have felt, very early in life, a great hatred for people who were wealthy and of high rank. As a youth, he talked a great deal about the rights of the lower classes, and the wrong doings of the upper classes; and he declared that the power of doing so much wrong should be taken away from the king and his nobles.

The poor people of France liked to hear such talk, for they had just reason to complain. Many of them came to look upon Robespierre as the champion of their rights, and to place much confidence in his ability to help them.

The revolutionists had come to think that the only remedy for their wrongs was the death of King Louis XVI; just as in England Cromwell and his friends, a hundred and fifty years earlier, had believed that the English people could gain their rights only by the death of Charles I.

Robespierre was determined that the king should be executed. He made a speech in which he said that France would be far better off without any king. He then went on to say that happiness and prosperity would return to the country if only Louis could be removed; and that the only way to remove him was to put him to death.

Most of the Assembly thought that the person of a king was sacred; and that if his life was taken, the curse of God would rest upon those who took it. Robespierre boldly denied this; and the people were delighted with his words. They named him "The Incorruptible;" and they almost worshiped him.

One day, when he was leaving the hall where the meetings of the Assembly were held, they placed a crown of oak leaves upon his head, unharnessed the horses from his carriage, and drew him to his home themselves. As they passed along the streets, they cried: "Behold the friend of the people! Behold the defender of liberty!"

The revolutionists raised an army of their own, placed a guard around the palace, and made the king a prisoner. Then they brought him to trial and charged him with being the cause of all the troubles that the people of France had suffered during his reign.

Three excellent lawyers were employed to defend him; and they spoke very strongly in his behalf. But on January 16, 1793, this mock court sentenced him to death.

After the death of Louis XVI, Robespierre became the absolute master of France; and he was so cruel that the period of his rule has been called "The Reign of Terror." People were afraid, when they rose in the morning, that they might be beheaded during the day; and when they went to bed they feared lest assassins might enter their rooms and kill them while they slept.

It is stated, on good authority, that the executions during Robespierre's rule averaged about thirty a day.

After a while people began to see that their condition had not improved. Everybody in Paris was extremely unhappy; and some did not hesitate to say that they were worse off under Robespierre than they had been under Louis XVI.

As Robespierre himself had taught the people that the death of the ruler was the great remedy for their troubles, many persons began to think that it would be the best thing for France if Robespierre himself should be put to death.

Arrest of Robespierre

A conspiracy was formed to bring Robespierre to trial; and one day a bold speaker arose in the Convention and openly blamed him for his cruelty.

Robespierre rose from his seat and was about to make a speech in his own defense; but the hall was filled with cries of "Down with the tyrant! Down with the tyrant!" and he fled from the building in great alarm.

In a few moments he was surrounded by the officers of the Convention. As they were about to seize him he tried to kill himself by firing a pistol at his head; but the ball only fractured his lower jaw.

Together with twenty of his friends he was executed on the same day on which he was arrested.

CHAPTER 26

Napoleon Bonaparte

(1769-1821)

THE home of Napoleon Bonaparte for the first ten years of his life was at Ajaccio (a yat' cho) on the island of Corsica. When ten years of age he was sent to a military school. At sixteen he entered the army.

When France was declared a republic he sided with the revolutionists. Some of the people of Paris did not like the idea of a republic, and about forty thousand of them marched through the streets to attack the Tuileries where the republican Convention was sitting.

The Convention had learned that an attack was to be made on them, and they had prepared to resist it. They had troops; but they needed a commander.

One of the members who knew Napoleon said, "I know just the man you want. He is a little Corsican officer and will not stand upon ceremony."

Napoleon was sent for and put in command. He led out their forces and many of the royalists were killed or wounded, and the rest fled. He had done his work well, and the Convention at once gave him a higher position

A French army, sent to attack the Austrians in North Italy was placed under his command. The soldiers were greatly dissatisfied because their pay was in arrears. Napoleon said to them, "I will lead you into the most fertile fields that the sun shines on. Rich provinces and great cities shall be your reward."

The Austrians posted themselves near a town called Lodi, on the bank of the River Adda. A bridge crossed the Adda into the town, and this bridge was first taken. Then Napoleon and General Lannes made a splendid charge and captured the town itself.

Four days later Napoleon entered Milan, and compelled that wealthy city to pay him nearly four million dollars. Mantua was also captured and the palaces of the dukes and nobles were plundered.

When peace was made Austria was obliged to surrender Belgium, Corfu and the Ionian Islands, and to liberate General Lafayette and other Frenchmen held in Austrian prisons.

Napoleon at School in Brienne

With French aid, republics were established in Switzerland, Naples, and Rome; and Napoleon then said: "If my voice has any influence England shall never have one hour's truce until she is destroyed."

But his next campaign was in Egypt, where he was again victorious. The English commander, Nelson, however, destroyed the ships in which the French soldiers were expecting to return; and so Napoleon, leaving fifteen thousand troops to hold possession of Egypt, marched the remainder of his army into Palestine.

He was successful in an attack on Jaffa. Then he proceeded northward to Acre, which was garrisoned by the Turks. After besieging this town for more than sixty days, he was compelled to withdraw.

Napoleon then returned to Egypt and found a great Turkish army just about to attack the troops he had left there; but he conquered them in a single battle and once more hastened back to France, where he was warmly welcomed by the people, and was the idol of the army.

At that time France was governed by five men who were called "The Directory," or ruling body of France. There was also a "Council of Five Hundred," something like our House of Representatives.

The Directory resigned; and since many of the Council of Five Hundred disliked him, Napoleon had them turned out of office.

Napoleon and two associates were then made rulers of France, under the title of Consuls; and, although he was known as the "First Consul," he was the real governor of the French nation.

One of the first things Napoleon did after being made First Consul, was to write a letter to George III, king of England, proposing that England and France should make peace. The English government replied that the easiest thing for France to do, if she desired peace with the other powers of Europe, would be to restore the royal family to the throne.

Napoleon then made his famous attack on Italy, which had been lost to France while he was in Egypt.

Sixty thousand men were ordered to cross the Alps. They were to go by four different passes and then to meet in Italy. Cannon had to be dragged over the snow; and sometimes a hundred men were required to handle a single large gun.

They passed the Monastery of St. Bernard and descended into Italy. A desperate battle was fought at Marengo; and, after a partial defeat, the French were again victorious.

The conqueror returned home in triumph, but his enemies attempted to assassinate him by exploding a barrel of gunpowder under his carriage. The carriage, however, had got safely past before the explosion took place.

This incident led to giving him still greater power, and Napoleon was from that time considered as the emperor of the French.

In 1801, the very next year after the victory at Marengo, British troops landed in Egypt, and in one short campaign drove the French out of that country.

When Napoleon heard that Egypt was lost, he said, "Well! There remains only the descent on Britain;" and in a short time one hundred and sixty thousand men were ready to invade England.

Napoleon in Egypt

An immense number of flat-bottomed boats were prepared to carry this force across the channel. But Lord Nelson was guarding the English coasts by day and by night. Napoleon knew that Nelson's guns would soon sink his boats; and so a treaty of peace was made in 1802, and the struggle with England was again postponed.

Napoleon was as great a tyrant as Louis XVI; and he tried to be as tyrannical in foreign countries as he was at home. The people of northern Italy were so alarmed by his victories at Lodi, Mantua, and Marengo, that they allowed him to take from them all independence and make their states a province of France. He treated Switzerland in the same way.

The peace between France and England lasted but one year, and then Napoleon again prepared for an invasion. A large army was assembled in camps along the coasts of France and Holland, but the French were again hindered from sailing by the vigilance of Nelson.

The coronation of the emperor and empress, on May 18, 1804, was a very grand affair; and the French people seemed to be well satisfied with their new rulers.

A few months later Napoleon went to Milan and there crowned himself "King of Italy" with the famous iron crown of Charlemagne. This angered the Austrians and Russians, and Russia and England became the allies of Austria.

Napoleon in Coronation Robes

Napoleon continued to wage war until his very name became a terror, and after his great victory at Austerlitz men feared him more and more. At the battle of Jena (ya' na), where he fought against the Prussians, he was again triumphant, and he carried himself as though he was the master of the world.

He divorced his wife Josephine, and married Maria Louisa, daughter of the Emperor of Austria.

Troubles again arose with Russia, and Napoleon's advisors tried to persuade him not to go to war; but he said, "The states of Europe must be melted into one nation, and Paris must be its capital."

The Russian army was only about half as large as that of the French. By a system of carefully arranged retreats it lured Napoleon and his men into the very heart of Russia.

Near Moscow a battle was fought which lasted all day, and neither party could claim the victory. Next morning the Russians had disappeared, and the French army entered the city and pillaged it. But so many fires occurred that Napoleon was obliged to leave the city just as the terrible Russian winter began.

Napoleon at the Battle of Jenna

When the French entered Moscow, over one hundred thousand soldiers answered the roll-call; but when they returned to France only twelve thousand were alive. It has been well said that "the fortunes of Napoleon were buried in the Russian snows."

England, Russia, Prussia, Sweden and Austria now declared war against him. He was defeated at Leipzig and again driven back into France. The allied armies pursued him, captured Paris, forced him to abdicate, and placed Louis XVIII on the throne. Napoleon was banished to a little island in the Mediterranean, called Elba.

Louis XVIII tried to govern as his brother had done before the revolution, and the French again became discontented. When, therefore, the news was heard that Napoleon had escaped from Elba and was again in France, the whole nation broke into the wildest rejoicing, and Napoleon was once more emperor.

Napoleon on Board the Bellerophon

He marched into Belgium, and there fought his last battle. He had a fine army, and the English and Prussian generals, Wellington and Blucher, were equally well equipped.

Napoleon managed to get between the English and Prussian armies. He defeated the Prussians on June 16, but in turn was beaten by the English. Then on the heights about Waterloo, the decisive battle was fought, June 18, 1815.

Both sides fought with great bravery. In front of the English was a sunken road cut into the hill like a ditch; and this was concealed from the French by a hedge.

Three thousand five hundred of the French cavalry plunged into this ditch, as they rode up rank after rank; and the survivors were compelled to ride over the struggling bodies of their comrades.

Then the English, drawn up in solid masses, received the French charge on the points of their bayonets, and, at the same time, poured a heavy fire into their broken ranks.

At about five in the afternoon Blucher appeared and united his troops with those of Wellington. Napoleon's famous "Old Guard" made a charge which Wellington himself said was "splendid;" but the French army was thrown into confusion and Wellington won the day.

A month later Napoleon went on board the Bellerophon, an English man-of-war, and surrendered himself to the captain. He was afterwards taken by the British to an island in the Atlantic Ocean, called St. Helena, and was kept a prisoner there until his death in 1821.

In 1840, the French government requested the English to allow them to bring his body to France.

In Paris the body was received by Louis Philippe, who was then king of France. More than a million people gathered in the streets through which the funeral procession passed; and thirty thousand were present at the funeral service, which closed with a requiem sung by three hundred voices.

CHAPTER 27

Horatio Nelson

(1758-1805)

HORATIO NELSON was born in 1758. At twelve years of age he asked permission to go to sea with an uncle named Suckling; but as his uncle did not sail that year, he was sent in charge of a friend, on a voyage to the West Indies.

It was not many days before the sailor boy knew the name of every rope on the ship, and the use of each. He could "box the compass," that is, repeat the names of all the thirty-two points backwards and forwards, and could tell in what direction the ship was sailing. When he returned to England he was fonder of the sea than ever.

Sometime after reaching home he heard that two ships of the navy were going to the North Pole, and he obtained permission to go with them.

The vessels after sailing far toward the north, were becalmed. The weather became very cold, and they were surrounded by great fields of ice.

One night, while they were frozen up in the ice fields, Nelson and one of his comrades stole away from their ship to attack a huge polar bear. Pretty soon they were missed; but although they were not far away a thick fog prevented those on board from seeing them The captain became alarmed, the signal for their return was fired, and Nelson, much disappointed; went back to the ship.

Fortunately, a wind soon sprang up from the east and a current drifted them into clear water. In due time they sighted "Old England" once more.

Nelson's next voyage was to the East Indies, and there he cruised about for eighteen months. The hot climate did not agree with him, and he was finally sent home; but on the voyage his health improved so much that when he reached England he was ready to go to sea again.

The Spaniards then claimed Central and South America; and England was at war with Spain. So a plan was proposed to seize that part of South America where the canal is now being cut to connect the Atlantic and Pacific Oceans.

There the Spaniards had two forts, and Nelson was sent to capture them. When he got near one of them he leaped ashore from his boat. He alighted on ground so soft that he sank into it and lost his shoes. But this did not stop him. Barefoot he led on his men and took one fort. The other was also soon taken; but the climate of the region was far more deadly than the guns of the Spaniards; and Nelson was obliged to return to England on sick leave.

It was three months before he was well enough to go to sea again. He was then appointed to the Albemarle, a vessel of twenty-eight guns. This was at the time that George III was trying to conquer the American colonies; and Nelson was sent to cruise in the waters of Canada and New England.

After the surrender of the British at Yorktown, Nelson wrote home: "I have closed the war without a fortune; but there is not a speck on my character."

After the execution of Louis XVI, England, as we have said, was at war with France, and Nelson was put in command of the Agamemnon, a ship of sixty-four guns.

The French, at about this time, took possession of the little island of Corsica on which Napoleon was born. They placed a garrison in a fortified town called Calvi; and the English laid siege to it. The Agamemnon was ordered to aid the land forces; and so Nelson took his men and guns ashore, and fought on the land.

Calvi was taken and Corsica was annexed to Great Britain; but for Nelson this battle proved a serious matter. A shot struck the ground near him and drove some sand and gravel into his eye. He thought, at first, that no great harm had been done; but the sight of the eye was lost.

A short time after this the English admiral under whom Nelson was serving, learned that a French fleet of twenty-two vessels, with over sixteen thousand men, was not far off. The English fleet consisted of only fifteen ships, with half as many men as the French. However, when they came in sight of the French they gave chase.

The Agamemnon with her sixty-four guns followed a French frigate of eighty-four, called the Ca Ira. Nelson was all alone, for the other ships of the

English fleet were several miles distant. Near the Ca Ira were three other French vessels of one hundred and thirty guns.

Nelson sailed close up to the big ship, and when about one hundred yards astern of her, suddenly ordered the helm to be put to the right, and fired his whole broadside—that is, all the guns on one side of his vessel. Then he ordered the helm hard to the left and started after the Frenchmen again; and when he came near he turned and fired another broadside.

This he did again and again for two hours and a quarter, always keeping out of the range of the enemy's guns. But so many other French ships came upon the scene that, fearing that they would prove too much for him, he sailed away and joined the English fleet.

Next morning the French fleet was again discovered about five miles away; but the Ca Ira had been so much injured that she had to be towed, and was only about three and a half miles distant.

Nelson attacked both the Ca Ira and the vessel which was towing her. The French fought gallantly, but the guns of the Agamemnon were so well aimed that the two French ships lost about three hundred men. Then both of them lowered their colors and surrendered.

Spain was now in alliance with France and fighting against England. Nelson attacked a Spanish frigate, and after conquering her had the captain brought on board his ship. Then four more Spanish vessels hove in sight and Nelson prudently sailed away. As soon as he reached a port, he gave the Spanish captain his liberty and sent him to his friends under a flag of truce.

Not long after this the English fleet of nineteen vessels was signaled to keep in line of battle all night. At daybreak a Spanish fleet of thirty-eight vessels was in sight. Sir John Jervis, finding that they were much scattered, ordered the English ships to sail in among them and attack them. Nelson was so much afraid that the Spanish ships would escape that he was soon engaged with seven Spanish vessels which had in all about six hundred guns.

Fortunately, two British vessels came up to the assistance of Nelson's ship. Both these ships were damaged by shots from the guns of the Spaniards; but at length Nelson managed to steer alongside of one of the Spanish vessels called the St. Nicholas, and he and his men boarded her.

The Spanish officers took refuge in the cabin, and fired at the boarding party through the windows; but the English forced the doors and the Spaniards surrendered their swords to Nelson.

Another Spanish vessel called the San Joseph lay close to the St. Nicholas; and the English, led by Nelson himself, forced her to surrender.

For his great bravery Nelson was made a Knight of the Bath, and so became Sir Horatio Nelson.

His next adventure was an attack upon Teneriffe; and there he was so severely injured in the right arm that he was obliged to have it amputated.

After recovering from his wound he was again placed in command. His vessel was the Vanguard. Napoleon was preparing his great expedition for the conquest of Egypt. Nelson sailed in search of the French and defeated them in the great battle of the Nile.

In this engagement he was again wounded, but not so seriously as was at first supposed.

After the battle he again returned to England. When he entered the harbor of Yarmouth every ship in port hoisted her colors; and in London he was drawn in triumph through the streets, and presented by the City Council with a gold-hilted sword studded with diamonds.

Napoleon was now at the height of his power. Denmark, Sweden and Russia had formed an alliance with France to try and take from England her sovereignty of the seas. The hostile fleets met off Copenhagen. Part of the English fleet was under Nelson's command. The admiral who was chief in command was at some distance when the battle began.

Thinking that the engagement was going against them, he gave the signal to cease firing; and the officer on Nelson's ship whose duty it was to watch for signals reported this to Nelson.

Nelson put his spyglass to his blind eye and looking toward the admiral's ship, said, "I really do not see the signal. Keep mine flying for closer battle."

Soon white flags were flying from the mastheads of many of the Danish vessels. Nelson had disobeyed orders, but he had gained the victory, and the enemy's fleet was disabled.

In 1804 France induced Spain to join her in a war against England, and a French and Spanish fleet sailed to the West Indies to attack the English and take possession there. But they returned to Europe, and Nelson learning that they were at Cadiz, went there to meet them.

Soon after his arrival, one of his frigates on the lookout, gave the signal that the French and Spanish fleet was coming out of port.

Nelson Boarding the St. Nicholas

Nelson in The Battle of Trafalgar

Just before they went into battle Nelson wrote a remarkable prayer and his last wishes. Then he ordered the famous signal to be made to the fleet, "England expects every man to do his duty."

The French had some Tyrolese riflemen on one of their ships; and a ball from one of their rifles struck Nelson on the shoulder. He fell. When taken up he said to his captain, "They have done for me at last, Hardy. My backbone is shot through." He knew that his wound was fatal, and when carried to the cockpit told the surgeon to attend to the others, "for" said he, "you can do nothing for me."

About an hour after he was wounded Captain Hardy came to see him.

"Well, Hardy," said he, "how goes the day with us?"

"Very well," said Hardy, "ten ships have struck." In less than an hour the captain returned and taking Nelson's hand, congratulated him on having gained a complete victory.

Presently the dying man said, "Kiss me, Hardy." Hardy knelt down and kissed his cheek: and Nelson said, "Now I am satisfied. Thank God I have done my duty." These words he repeated several times; and they were his last.

Thus Admiral Nelson, perhaps the greatest of England's naval commanders died on his good ship "Victory," in Trafalgar Bay, on October 21, 1805.

His body was carried back to England, and was buried with great pomp in St. Paul's Cathedral in London.

CHAPTER 28

Thaddeus Kosciusko

(1746–1817)

AMERICANS will never cease to honor the memory of the Polish patriot, Thaddeus Kosciusko (kos si us' ko). In his early manhood he was one of the noble band of liberty-loving foreigners who came to the United States and aided the American patriots in their struggle for independence.

Kosciusko was born in Poland in 1746. After a long and thorough course of study in the best military schools of Europe, he was appointed a captain in the Polish army. When the American revolution began, he determined to take part in it. He came to the United States and sought General Washington, who was commander-in-chief of the American army.

"General," he said, when he stood before Washington, "I have come to offer myself as a volunteer to fight for American independence."

"You are heartily welcome, captain," replied Washington, warmly shaking the hand of Kosciusko. "The patriot cause has need of the services of everyone who is willing to aid it. What can you do?"

"Try me," said Kosciusko modestly.

Washington smiled.

"I will try you, captain," he said cordially, "and I do not doubt that you will perform valuable service."

Kosciusko was appointed colonel of engineers, and soon showed by his skill in constructing fortifications that he could, indeed, render valuable service to the American army. He was subsequently made one of Washington's staff officers and served with the great commander for some time.

"Never have I known better or more faithful service from anyone," said Washington once when speaking of Kosciusko's work as a staff officer. "He was prompt, diligent, full of enthusiasm, while at the same time he was a man of large education and accomplishments. I regarded him almost as a younger brother and trusted him with my most important plans."

Toward the close of the war, Kosciusko was honored with the public thanks of the Continental Congress for his gallant deeds. He was appointed brigadier general, and for some months commanded a large force of the American army.

When the revolution ended, Kosciusko went back to Poland, proud to have taken part in the patriotic struggle. His countrymen welcomed him home with enthusiasm; and later he was made major general in the Polish army.

Kosciusko

In 1791, the Poles were forced to resist an invasion of their country by the Russians and Prussians. Kosciusko took part in the war, and on two occasions by skillful management saved the Polish force from entire destruction.

At the battle of Dubienka, with only about four thousand men, he kept at bay a Russian army of twenty thousand, and finally made his retreat without great loss. The Poles were generally outnumbered by the Russians and they fought gallantly; but they were completely overpowered. Russia and Prussia both annexed large parts of Poland.

Kosciusko At Raclawice

This annexation is known as the second partition of Poland. The first partition had taken place twenty years before, when Austria, Russia, and Prussia each took parts of the little kingdom.

In 1794 the Poles were so angry at the loss of their country that they took up arms once more.

A revolt was secretly planned, and on a certain day in the spring of 1794, Kosciusko suddenly appeared in the city of Cracow.

"The Russians must be driven from Poland; they must not rule our fair land," said Kosciusko to those of his countrymen who assembled at his call. "We can free ourselves from Russian slavery if we will fight."

The Poles hastily armed themselves, many with nothing but scythes, and advanced to meet the Russian army. After a sharp contest the enemy was driven out of Cracow.

A week later, at Raclawice (rat sla vit' se), a Polish army of five thousand, led by Kosciusko, routed a great force of Russians, and returned triumphantly to Cracow. The rebellion went on for several months with some success.

On October 10, 1794, an immense force of Russians advanced against the Poles. The little army of patriots numbered only four thousand. The Poles were defeated with heavy loss; and Kosciusko, fighting desperately, fell from his horse severely wounded.

He was made prisoner by the Russians, and taken to St. Petersburg, where he suffered a rigorous imprisonment. The Russian general, Suwaroff, captured Warsaw, and the kingdom of Poland came to an end; for now Russia, Prussia and Austria took to themselves all that remained of the Polish territory.

When Kosciusko had been in confinement two years, the czar gave him his liberty. "You are an enemy of Russia;" said the czar to him, "but you have shown great heroism; and I cannot help admiring a brave man."

The czar seeing that Kosciusko had no sword, offered him one.

"I have no need of a sword," said Kosciusko. "I have no country now to defend."

Immediately after his release from the Russian prison, Kosciusko went to England and then came to the United States. The Americans received him with great honor, and Congress gave him a liberal pension for his services in the Revolutionary War.

For some years afterwards he lived in France. Toward the close of his life he made his home in Switzerland, where he engaged in agricultural pursuits.

He died in 1817 in consequence of a fall from a horse.

His body was taken to Cracow and buried in the cathedral near the graves of other Polish patriots.

After the burial, the Polish people brought earth from all the battlefields on which Kosciusko had fought for Poland, and erected, near Cracow, a great mound, one hundred and fifty feet high, in honor of their hero.

CHAPTER 29

Abraham Lincoln

(1809-1865)

ABRAHAM LINCOLN, the sixteenth president of the United States, was the son of poor parents, and his childhood and youth were full of trial and hardship.

His father, Thomas Lincoln, was a pioneer farmer in Kentucky; and there, in a one-roomed log cabin of the poorer sort, Abraham Lincoln was born on February 12, 1809.

His mother was Nancy, the daughter of Joseph Hanks, a neighbor who was also trying to earn a livelihood out of the soil. Abraham had also one sister, of whom not much has been recorded.

As there was little to encourage his stay in Kentucky, Abraham's father moved into Indiana, and built a log cabin in the midst of the forest at Pigeon Creek. Here most of Lincoln's boyhood was passed.

In 1818, Mrs. Lincoln died, and Abraham Lincoln was left motherless.

Eighteen months later his father married Mrs. Sarah Bush Johnston, a widow who had been a neighbor in Kentucky. She was a good woman and treated Abraham with the same care and tenderness which she showed to her own children.

Abraham Lincoln formed a strong attachment for his stepmother which lasted all through his life. She was really able to do more for him than his own mother had been. He was not only better clothed and better fed; but he also had considerable help in his struggle for an education.

By the time he was ten he was working hard to help his father to clear some land and turn a little piece of the forest into a farm. He had little or no schooling. He once said, later on in life, that he did not think that all his schooling as a lad amounted to more than six months.

Birthplace of Abraham Lincoln

He learned to write by using a charred stick for a pencil, and a piece of board for a slate. There were no books in his home excepting a Bible, a catechism and a spelling book.

But he would walk miles to borrow a book, and he read with great care everything that he could find. He thus gathered a store of information that was of service to him throughout his wonderful career.

At sixteen years of age he had almost reached the height of six feet and four inches for which he was noted in after years.

His bodily strength was very great, and his services were very much in demand. He did everything he could to help his parents.

In 1830 the Lincoln family moved into Illinois and from that time their fortunes began to improve.

Lincoln was now twenty-one. One who knew him well at that time, thus describes his personal appearance: "He was tall, angular, and ungainly, and wore trousers made of flax and tow, cut tightly at the ankles and loosely at the knees. He was very poor but was welcome in every house in the neighborhood."

He built a flatboat, with his father's consent, and carried a load of farm produce down the river to market. It was on this trip that he earned his first dollar by carrying two gentlemen and their trunks out to a steamer on the Ohio, a fact of which he was very proud and of which he often spoke in after years.

He afterwards made other trips as a boatman and was very successful in them. It was on one of these trips that he witnessed, in New Orleans, the brutality of the slave trade. This led him to say, "If ever I get a chance to hit that institution, I'll hit it hard."

He next entered the employ of a Mr. Offutt who put him in charge of a general store at New Salem. While tending this store, Lincoln once sold to a woman goods for which she paid the amount of two dollars, six and a quarter cents. He discovered later that a mistake had been made, and that the store owed the customer the six and a quarter cents. After he had closed the store that night, he walked several miles in the darkness to return the amount.

At another time a woman bought a pound of tea. Lincoln discovered the next morning that a smaller weight was on the scales. He at once weighed out the remainder and walked some distance before breakfast to deliver it.

It was by such deeds as these that he earned the name of "Honest Abe." He gained the good will of his neighbors who called upon him to settle their disputes, and always found him fair and upright in his decisions.

Misfortune overtook Mr. Offutt and Lincoln entered the service of the state of Illinois in what is known as the Black Hawk War. He was elected captain of the company, but neither he nor his men were called upon to do any actual fighting.

At the close of the war he returned to New Salem and was urged to become a member of the legislature of Illinois; but he failed to be elected.

Like Washington he took up the business of a surveyor. In 1833 he was made postmaster of New Salem. In the following year, 1834, another election of the members of the state legislature took place, and this time he was successful and became a member for Sangamon County.

The two political parties were then known as the Democrats and the Whigs, and Lincoln belonged to the Whigs.

He was still so poor that he was obliged to borrow money with which to purchase suitable clothing before he could take his seat in the House.

His entering the legislature was an important event in his life. The capital of the state was soon afterwards changed from Vandalia to Springfield; and Lincoln who was rapidly rising into fame took up the study of law.

As a lawyer he was decidedly successful. He formed several partnerships with lawyers of eminence, and his days of biting poverty were over.

He still continued his general studies and became one of the best-informed men in the state. He gave his first legal fee to his stepmother in the shape of one hundred and sixty acres of land, in memory of her great kindness to him as a boy.

In November 1842, Abraham Lincoln married Miss Mary Todd, of Lexington, Kentucky, and the next ten years were the happiest of his whole life. In 1846 he was elected a member of the United States Congress. He took his seat in the House of Representatives at Washington on December 6th of that year.

His first important speech in Congress was one in which he denounced the war then being carried on between the United States and Mexico; a speech in which he dealt the pro-slavery party a severe blow.

At the end of his first term in Congress Mr. Lincoln determined not to seek re-election. He therefore returned to Springfield and resumed the practice of law.

When, in 1854, a bill was passed which put aside the Missouri Compromise and gave greater powers to the friends of slavery, Lincoln again entered politics. He became a candidate for the Illinois legislature and was elected.

Mr. Stephen A. Douglas was then at the height of his power and was bitterly opposed to Lincoln.

In 1860, with Douglas as his most formidable competitor, Mr. Lincoln was elected president; and in February 1861, he left Springfield for Washington and was duly inaugurated in March of that year.

In the election of Abraham Lincoln as president the South feared that the institution of slavery was in the gravest danger; and they put forth every possible effort for its defense.

Some of the Southern states voted to secede from the Union. Fort Sumter was fired upon, and the terrible Civil War began.

Lincoln called for men, and readily obtained them. It is to the honor of Mr. Douglas that when he saw the real danger in which the country stood, he acknowledged himself in the wrong and became one of Lincoln's friends and supporters.

This war, sometimes called the "War of the Union," lasted from 1861 to 1865. It was the saddest event in the history of our land; and every American boy and girl should make a careful study of its details from the fall of Fort Sumter to the surrender of General Lee at Appomattox.

Reading the Emancipation Proclaimation

These were trying days for President Lincoln; and at times his sufferings were intense. But he never flinched from what he felt to be his duty; and he was warmly supported by the generals, the army, and the people of the North.

During the progress of the war, after due warning, he issued his famous Emancipation Proclamation; and on January 1, 1863, most of the slaves in the South were declared free.

In 1864, the year before the close of the war, Abraham Lincoln was again elected president; and on March 4, 1865, he entered upon his second term of office. His majority at his second election was the largest ever given to any president up to that time.

When the war closed there was great rejoicing; and on April 11, two days after Lee's surrender, Lincoln made a speech in Congress in which he strongly urged that the states which had seceded should be treated with leniency and restored to their proper relations to the central government as quickly and as quietly as possible.

On April 14, 1865, the fourth anniversary of the fall of Fort Sumter, a general holiday was observed; and in the evening the President attended a special performance in Ford's theatre.

During the progress of the performance a retired actor gained access to the president's box and, placing a pistol over Lincoln's chair, shot him through the head.

The assassin escaped amid the general confusion, but was discovered, a few days later, in lower Maryland while hiding in a barn. He refused to surrender and was shot dead by one of the soldiers who had been sent to capture him.

CHAPTER 30

Garibaldi

(1807-1882)

GIUSEPPE GARIBALDI, a descendant of an old family of Lombards of North Italy, was born in Nice, on July 4, 1807.

At an early age he became an expert swimmer, and it is recorded that while still a lad he saved several persons from drowning.

He had an excellent mother, and his love for her was both tender and true; and she seems to have been instrumental in developing in him that strong patriotic feeling which formed the leading feature in his character.

It was under the direction of his mother, with the assistance of the village priest as schoolmaster, that he received his education.

His father was a seaman, and young Garibaldi accompanied him on several of his voyages, particularly to Rome and Constantinople.

By the time Garibaldi reached the age of twenty-four he had become warmly interested in the revolutionary movements of "Young Italy." His interest was greatly quickened through his becoming acquainted with Mazzini (mat zeé nee), who was just then preparing to invade Italy by sea.

The effort was unsuccessful, and Garibaldi hastily left the country and thus found himself an exile at the very beginning of his career. He took refuge in Marseilles, and afterwards joined the French navy.

As soon as he could get himself free from his entanglements he started on a sea voyage; and in 1836 we find him in Rio de Janeiro where he remained for about twelve years. These years were filled with romantic adventures, from some of which he barely escaped with his life.

Garibaldi and His Son

Rio Grande do Sul, one of the states of Brazil, possessing a vast territory, was at war with the Brazilian emperor, and Garibaldi threw in his lot with the revolutionists.

He first took command of a privateer, a small boat with only twelve men as crew. But a little later he was successful in seizing, as a prize, a much larger and better equipped vessel; and although not always successful in his encounters with the Brazilians he began to make himself felt as one of the factors to be dealt with in the war.

He passed over into the Argentine territory, and there fell into the hands of a brutish Spanish American who struck him across the face with a horse-whip, and who also caused him to suffer several hours of torture on the rack, after which he was cast into a dungeon.

Through the kindness of Madame Alleman, whom Garibaldi afterwards spoke of as "an angel of charity," his sufferings were not so intense as they otherwise might have been. Shortly afterwards, through the intervention of the governor he escaped from his tormentor.

On leaving the Argentine territory he crossed over again into Rio Grande and devoted himself anew to the cause of the revolutionists.

This time he met with better success, fighting many battles, sometimes with only a handful of men. The difficulties he met with were tremendous; but he never lost his courage, and showed so much skill and such strong personality as gave great authority to his counsels. He also softened the stern discipline under which the soldiers had fretted for years; and this made him popular with the army.

In a hurricane off the coast of Santa Catharina he was wrecked; and while detained there he met Anita, the talented woman who became his wife. She was a woman of heroic mold, and proved herself both true and helpful in all the hardships which befell him.

After the defeat of the revolutionists at the battle of Las Austras, Garibaldi seems to have grown discouraged as to the outcome of the war. He therefore bade farewell to his friends at Rio Grande and settled for a while in Montevideo.

At Montevideo he became a teacher of mathematics in one of the city schools; but the life of a teacher was too tame for a man of his adventurous spirit and he soon gave up his position and again entered upon the life of a soldier.

Some men who had become jealous of his successes in Rio Grande now plotted to have him assassinated; but in this they failed.

He was then put in charge of a small squadron and sent out to meet a much superior force, in the hope that he might be destroyed. But he won such glory in the battle of San Antonio as to earn for himself the proud title of "the Hero of Montevideo."

Through all his wanderings and adventures his heart remained true to the cause of his native country; and after an absence of over twelve years he decided to return to Italy.

With great difficulty he procured the money for his voyage, and he landed at Nice with his wife and a few faithful comrades in 1848.

On his arrival Garibaldi offered his services to the Italian government, but they were refused. Finally, the government of Lombardy gave him command of a small body of volunteers.

When Rome was attacked by the French, the Italians, regardless of party, gathered their forces about Garibaldi and drove the French back.

But the Italians suffered a terrible defeat in a three months' siege of Rome a little later on, and many valuable lives were lost.

The French took possession of the city; and Garibaldi, with a few devoted volunteers, set out to join the attack then being made on Austria. He and his followers were met on all sides by the overwhelming forces of Austria and were compelled to disband and flee to the woods.

Garibaldi sought shelter for his brave wife Anita; but she was unable to endure the hardships which followed and died in the arms of her husband.

Our heart-broken hero again became a wanderer. A friend supplied him with means to reach Tunis, and obtained for him a pension, which he gladly accepted.

Garibaldi again crossed the ocean, this time to the United States. He became a successful businessman in New York, where he remained until his return to Europe in 1855.

When he reached home he purchased a part of the islet of Caprera on the coast of Sardinia; and built a little home which he called "The Hermitage."

Four years later he was again called to defend the cause of Italy. He was given command of a regiment, and again went forth to meet the Austrians whom he defeated at Varese. He continued in the service until the peace of Villa-franca, to which Napoleon was a party; and this treaty brought the long struggle for Italian independence to a successful close.

Victor Emmanuel was now on the throne of Italy, and Garibaldi, who was popularly known as "the hero of the red shirt," was warmly welcomed by him.

It was in Victor Emmanuel that the hopes of the patriots now centered for the freedom of Italy, and they were not disappointed; for by the wise policy of Count Cavour, the prime minister, and the many victories of Garibaldi, it was established on a firm basis.

After meeting Victor Emmanuel and hailing him as king, Garibaldi retired to his hermitage; but a great part of Italy still longed to possess Rome as its capital.

The French upheld the power of the Pope; but the Franco-Prussian war of 1870 caused France to withdraw her troops from Rome.

When the French republic was established, Victor Emmanuel was officially told that France would no longer uphold the Papal power; and the Italian government informed the Pope that Rome would thereafter be considered a part of the kingdom of Italy.

On July 2, 1872, Victor Emmanuel took up his residence in Rome, and the palace of the Vatican became the Pope's place of residence.

In 1875 Garibaldi became a member of the Italian parliament. Titles and honors were offered him but he declined to accept them.

His health was rapidly failing. So he retired again to his hermitage, where he died on June 2, 1882, at the age of seventy-five.

CHAPTER 31

William Ewart Gladstone (1809-1898)

WILLIAM EWART GLADSTONE was born of Scotch parents, and he was one of the very few Scotchmen who have taken a prominent part in British statecraft.

He was sent to the great public school at Eton when twelve years of age. There he was always noted for his good behavior and for his regular attendance at the chapel services. It is also recorded of him that he could recite more verses of Scripture than any other boy in the school.

The character of Mr. Gladstone is very hard to analyze because of its many-sidedness; and for that reason he was often misunderstood and lost many friends.

He graduated from Christ Church College, Oxford, when twenty-two years of age, having won the highest honors the college could bestow.

An account of his appearance, published at the time of his graduation says, "In features he is handsome; his face is bold and masculine; his eyes are of piercing luster; and his hair, which he tosses back in debate, is like a lion's mane. He speaks five languages, is an excellent tenor singer, is on more than speaking terms with many of the greatest men in England, and besides all this he is rich in English gold."

His influence at college was so abiding that Cardinal Manning has said that, "There was less wine drunk at Oxford during the forties than would have been the case if Gladstone had not been there in the thirties."

It appears to have been his intention to become a clergyman of the English church, and he studied with this object in view.

His father had other plans for him and half forced him into politics; so that immediately on leaving college he ran for Parliament, was elected, and at once made his influence felt in the House of Commons.

For more than sixty years thereafter, he was one of the powers to be reckoned with on all questions connected with the English government.

At thirty-three years of age he was a member of the British Cabinet; but three years later his absolute honesty compelled him to resign from the Ministry. His opponents said, "Gladstone is an extinct volcano." But they were continually discovering that a volcano is a difficult thing to subdue.

In his home life he was gentle, amiable and hospitable. His social instincts were large and his disposition was kindly. He was always true to his friends, and they revered him to a point little short of idolatry.

Gladstone

He delivered his maiden speech in Parliament on a subject connected with the great movement for the emancipation of the West Indian slaves; but he seemed to have confined himself mainly to a defense of the manner in which his father's estates were managed, the course of the debate having brought out some charges against the management of the elder Gladstone's possessions in one of the West Indian Islands. In January 1835, Sir Robert Peel appointed Gladstone to the office of a Junior Lord of the Treasury. In the next year, Peel, who was quick to appreciate the great abilities and the sound commercial knowledge of his new recruit, gave him the important post of Undersecretary for the Colonies.

Peel went out of office very soon after he had made Mr. Gladstone Undersecretary for the colonies. Lord John Russell brought forward a series of motions on the subject of the Irish Church, and Peel being defeated, resigned. It is almost needless to say that Gladstone went with him. In 1841, Sir Robert Peel again came into power, and Gladstone was given a seat in his Cabinet as President of the Board of Trade.

At the general election in 1847, Mr. Gladstone, still accepted as a Tory, was chosen one of the representatives of the University of Oxford.

Up to the time of the movement which led to the abolition of the Corn Laws, Mr. Gladstone had been a Tory of a rather old-fashioned school. The Corn Law agitation probably first set him thinking over the possible defects of the social and legislative system, and showed him the necessity for reform at least in one direction. At the death of Sir Robert Peel, in 1850, Mr. Gladstone lost a trusted leader, and a dear friend. But the loss of his leader brought Gladstone himself more directly to the front.

It was not until after Peel's death that he compelled the House of Commons and the country to recognize in him a supreme master of parliamentary debate. The first really great speech made by Mr. Gladstone in Parliament was made in the debate on Mr. Disraeli's budget in the winter of 1852, the first session of the new Parliament.

Mr. Disraeli sat down at two o'clock in the morning, and then Mr. Gladstone rose to reply to him. Most men in the House, even on the opposition side, were filled with the belief that it would be impossible to make any real impression on the House after such a speech as that of Mr. Disraeli. Long before Mr. Gladstone had concluded, everyone admitted that the effect of Mr. Disraeli's speech had been outdone, and Gladstone became fully recognized as the man of the hour; a man to rank with Bolingbroke, Pitt, and Fox.

With that speech began the long parliamentary duel between these two great masters of debate, Mr. Gladstone and Mr. Disraeli, which was carried on for four and twenty years.

On the fall of the short-lived Tory administration, Lord Aberdeen came into office. He formed the famous Coalition Ministry. Lord Palmerston took what most people would have though

ht the uncongenial office of Home Secretary. Mr. Gladstone, who with other of the "Peelites," as they were called, had joined the new administration, was made Chancellor of the Exchequer.

His speech on the introduction of his first budget was waited for with great interest, but none of those who listened to it would have wished it to be shortened by a sentence. A budget speech by Mr. Gladstone was a triumph in the realm of fine arts. The Crimean War broke up the Coalition Ministry; but the year 1859 saw Lord Palmerston back in office, and Mr. Gladstone in his old place as Chancellor of the Exchequer.

The death of Lord Palmerston, in 1865, called Lord Russell to the position of prime minister, and made Mr. Gladstone leader of the House of Commons.

Mr. Gladstone's mind had long been turning in the direction of an extension, or rather expansion, of the suffrage. It was assumed by everyone that Lord Russell and Mr. Gladstone being now at the head of affairs, a reform bill would be sure to come. It did come in 1866, a very moderate and cautious bill, enlarging the area of the franchise in boroughs and counties. The Conservative party opposed it. The bill was defeated, and the Liberal statesman went out of office.

Somewhere about this time the attention of Mr. Gladstone began to be attracted to the condition of Ireland. The distress and distracted state of Ireland, the unceasing popular agitation and discontent, and the Fenian insurrection, with its contemplated attack on Chester Castle, led Mr. Gladstone to the conviction that the time had come when statesmanship must seek through Parliament for some process of remedy.

In 1868 the Liberals returned to power, and Mr. Gladstone became prime minister. In his first session of government he disestablished and disendowed the state church in Ireland. In the next session he passed a measure which for the first time recognized the right of the Irish tenant to the value of the improvements he had himself made at his own cost and labor. Never probably was there such a period of energetic reform in almost every direction as that which set in when Mr. Gladstone became prime minister.

It was also at this time, and quite largely through Mr. Gladstone's efforts, that the first system of national education was established in England. The Ballot Act was passed for the protection of the voters so that they might vote as they wished without having to suffer painful consequences after the election was over. These two measures have been of great value to the English people and they prize them very highly.

For awhile Mr. Gladstone occupied himself in literary and historical studies, and published quite a number of essays and pamphlets. But even in his literary career Mr. Gladstone would appear to have always kept glancing at the House of Commons, as Charles V in his monastery kept his eyes on the world of politics outside.

The atrocious conduct of the Turkish officials in Bulgaria aroused his generous anger, and he flung down his books and rushed out from his study to preach a crusade against the Ottoman power in Europe.

It was an unpropitious hour at which to return to office. There were troubles in Egypt; there was impending war in the Sudan and in South Africa. There was something like an agrarian revolution going on in Ireland; and the Home Rule party in the House of Commons was under new, resolute, and uncompromising leadership.

He was out of office in a few months; and then the general elections came on. These elections were to give the first opportunity to the newly-made voters under Mr. Gladstone's latest reform act; and these voters sent him back into office and he once again took the helm and strove to guide the ship of state through the troubled seas which beat upon it from every point of the compass.

Under his leadership a home-rule bill for Ireland was passed by the Commons in spite of most bitter opposition. It was rejected almost unanimously by the House of Lords.

But time was beginning to tell upon the "Grand Old Man;" for he was now eighty-four years old and felt himself unequal to the gigantic struggle of the hour. He therefore resigned his offices and retired into private life in March 1894.

Mr. Gladstone sat in Parliament for sixty-three years; and for twenty-six years he was the leader of his party.

The three most notable acts of his political career were, the Disestablishment of the Irish Church, in 1866; his opposition to England's support of Turkey in 1876; and his work in favor of Home Rule for Ireland in 1886; while he had also much to do with the two great Reform Bills of 1855 and 1884.

Mr. Gladstone affords a splendid example of a man who devoted his life to the political service of his country, and still preserved his moral and religious character.

He died at his home, Hawarden Castle, in 1898.

CHAPTER 32

Count Von Bismarck

(1815-1898)

OTTO EDUARD LEOPOLD BISMARCK was born on the estate of Schonhausen, near Stendal, in Prussian Saxony, on April 1, 1815.

His ancestors had been famous both in war and in diplomatic circles for several generations.

They were descended from the Prussian nobility; and his grandfather had held the office of Privy Counsellor to Frederick the Great.

At the age of six he entered a boarding school in Berlin, where he tells us they "served elastic meat, always accompanied with parsnips."

When he was twelve, he came under the influence of Dr. Prevost who did much for the broadening of his mind and the strengthening of his character.

During his vacations he developed his powers of endurance by participating in manly sports; and then, at the age of seventeen, he entered the University of Gottingen for the purpose of studying law.

As a student he was not a brilliant success. He did not hold himself strictly to the prescribed studies of his course. During the first year of his university life he fought twenty-eight duels; in one of these he was wounded on the left cheek and he carried the scar left by the wound all through his later life.

On leaving Gottingen, in 1833, he went to Berlin. After a couple of years of study there he received the diploma necessary to enable him to enter upon a professional career, but decided to devote his time to the care of his estate.

When thirty-two years of age he was elected a member of the General Diet. He at once began to impress the people with his great tact and forethought, and each year their confidence in him was deepened.

He exercised a large amount of outward patience toward those who opposed him; but he was simply awaiting the time when he could strike such decisive blows as would assure his ultimate success. This was one of the marked characteristics of his whole career.

Napoleon III and Bismarck at Sedan

It would seem that from the very beginning of his political life the people decided to take him just as he was; and they grew to be very fond of him.

His aim was to preserve the peace of Europe. With great skill he avoided trouble both for himself and for his countrymen; and he quickly made for himself a name both at home and abroad.

His early life was lived among the Prussians, but he became objectionable to them because of his desire for power.

At the first Prussian Parliament in which he sat, in 1847, he said in one of his speeches, "Away with the cities. I hope to see them all leveled to the ground;"

and these words had in them the ring of that social hatred which he always showed toward the liberal class.

He followed very closely in the footprints of Garibaldi in the struggle for the unity and independence of Italy; and it would seem to be equally certain that Bismarck's methods were also followed by Garibaldi on several occasions.

There were many non-Prussians who greatly admired Bismarck on account of his endeavors for German unity; but the people in the southern part of Germany were equally strong in their dislike for him.

Through many discouragements he continued to press calmly onward in what he felt to be the path of duty, and for over twenty years his career was unusually prosperous.

King William I of Prussia Proclaimed German Emperor

At different periods Bismarck was appointed ambassador to Austria, Russia, and France. In 1862, at the age of forty-seven, he became Minister of the King's Household, and also Minister of Foreign Affairs in Prussia.

The brother of the king was very much opposed to Bismarck's plan of excluding Austria from a place in the remodeled German Confederation. Even the queen looked upon this measure with fear, for she had been brought up under the principles of constitutional government.

The Princess Royal of England also showed a bitter spirit toward him, for she was anxious for the future of her children. But King William was a true friend to him, and Bismarck never regretted that he had placed confidence in the king's faithfulness.

In May 1866, a fanatic by the name of Kohn attempted to kill Bismarck; and there were some who openly expressed their regret that the attempt was not successful.

Bismarck devoted his efforts to two main purposes, to transfer Austria to a position in the East, and to give to Germany political unity under Prussia.

Bismarck at Versailles

He seems to have felt that if Austria were removed from her position within the federal body, she would become a permanent ally of the New Germany; and that, in time, it would be better for her own interests and for those of Europe.

Bismarck had two powerful antagonists in the persons of Napoleon III of France and Earl Russell of England; and some thought he was working to bring about the union of France and Russia. But he was only measuring the men with whom he had to do and studying out the plans he had in mind for the strengthening and consolidation of the German empire; and it has well been said, "It was Bismarck's constant misfortune to be misunderstood."

In the Franco-Prussian War of 1870-71, France was severely humbled; but what was of most interest to Bismarck was that it caused such national enthusiasm among the Germans that, at Versailles, in January 1871, the New German Empire was established with the king of Prussia as its leader.

It was also at this time that Bismarck was raised to the rank of prince.

On May 10, 1871, at the Treaty of Frankfort, France was obliged to give to Germany the province of Alsace, the greater part of Lorraine, and to pay an indemnity of five billion francs.

Bismarck now paid close attention to the interests of the "fatherland." Germany was a federation, not greatly admired by some of the German people themselves; but accepted because it avoided making any radical changes in political affairs.

Under Bismarck's skillful management, it had been made so strong a power that war with France was no longer dreaded.

Germany is also indebted to Bismarck for its colonial policy; and although there are but few German colonial ports, they command a very large trade. But it required all his tact and perseverance to make the people see the advantages which this policy would bring them.

After the death of William I, Prince Frederick ascended the throne; but he lived only a short time.

When William II came into power it was soon apparent that the emperor and the chancellor were not in accord; and Bismarck resigned his office on March 20, 1890 and retired to private life.

The emperor presented him with the Dukedom of Lauenburg; and he took great interest in all the affairs of the German nation until his death in 1898.

Appendix: Impact of the Industrial Revolution

The Industrial Revolution began in the Eighteenth Century and gave rise to many of the modern amenities that humans enjoy today. With the development of machine-driven tools and factories, the economic growth of the urban cities became the predominant places for humans to migrate to in order to find work and to survive. Inventions of the Industrial Revolution include electricity, the cotton gin, and major transportation developments such as the transcontinental railroad.

Although the railroad has largely gone out of commission, the ability to mass produce vehicles fabricated from factories has taken its place. Electricity is still a modern amenity that most American households have, and the cotton gin helped to revolutionize the clothing and fabrication industries, which has paved the path for factories to develop and produce mass quantities of clothing and textiles.

There are some pitfalls to the Industrial Revolution; one such being the over-crowding of cities. Cities can't sustain the massive influx of people, and the employment opportunities in the Industrial Revolution and extending to modern times, have seen the results of the over-crowding. The homeless populace and the impoverished lend to the rise in crime rates within the over-crowded cities. The rise in pollution from these cities has had a lasting effect on modern times; such that it has seen the rise in global warming, as well as the pollution of the oceans and deforestation of the rainforests to accommodate such large populations.

Machine-driven factories were such a staple of the Industrial Revolution that the economic boom within the participating countries shaped the way for the supply and demand of the modern economy. The poor working conditions and inhumane way that workers were treated, also led to the revolutionization of labor laws, which saw the abolishment of child labor and the fair incorporation of laws, such as healthy and reasonable working hours like the nine to five hours.

With the economy growing in the Industrial Revolution and the uniform hours of work being imparted by major corporations on behalf of human rights, even simple things like rush-hour traffic have reverberated through to modern times. Rush-hour traffic begins two hours before nine in the morning, and is felt between the hours of four to six in the evening when the working-class would be done with work for the day.

Perhaps one of the greatest inventions of the Industrial Revolution was the invention of the automobile. It is debated who can be credited with the invention of the automobile, but it is believed to be Karl Benz from Germany in 1885. The invention of the automobile saw public transportation redefined, in that it took the place of the transcontinental railroad, to transcontinental highways, and also saw a rise in vehicle laws, rules, restrictions and expectations regarding driving on the road. The speed of travel was significantly increased because of the automobile. Where trains and boats once were the dominating modes of transportation, people were able to travel much quicker and with more direct routes to their destinations.

Modern medicine is a huge force in not only the Industrial Revolution and how it shaped modern times, but the ability to mass produce large quantities of pharmaceuticals and surgical equipment, shaped the infrastructure of modern medicine, in that it caters to large masses of people. The complaint often heard in modern times is that the pharmaceutical companies are the driving forces behind the world of medicine, and this is owed in part to the Industrial Revolution and the invention of the machine which is able to produce mass quantities of product, and subsequently dictate the economy regarding the products.

The economy in the Industrial Revolution was what defined and founded the creation of a middle-class. The middle-class were the workers, the tradesmen and women who were needed for manpower in the machine factories, but not just in the factories, in other industries as well, such as mining, transportation and agriculture. The middle-class comprised almost 90% of the population, but the lives of the middle-class people were challenging, hard and undervalued. The poor working conditions and inhumane rights towards slaves, children, women and even middle-class men, were such that it led to not just the revolution of the industries, but the revolt against them.

The Industrial Revolution saw a rise in increased labor laws and political rights. Because the people were treated so poorly, so eventually they were left with nothing to lose except their lives. Labor expectations were detrimental to the working-class, and health and the quality of living were at an all-time low. In addition to labor laws being enacted, and the working-classes going on strike to demand fair compensation and rights for the dangerous and grueling work they did, people discovered that by joining together, they could demand fair political rights as well. The politicians of the Industrial Revolution often capitalized on the monetary benefits of the economy, leaving the working-class barely able to sustain a living, whilst they themselves reaped the benefits of the arduous labor. Political movements began in the Industrial Revolution on behalf of the populace, and this also included the abolition of slavery.

Slave labor was relied heavily upon, until the populace began to commiserate with such poor qualities of life and health. The abolition of slavery came in a time when the people were demanding fair and reasonable labor and political laws for themselves on behalf of humanity, and this lent credence to the ideology that slavery itself was inhumane. In modern times, the push for fair and just laws regarding the economy, politics, social reform and cultural reform, are a result of these pushes on behalf of the Industrial Revolution.